MODERN-DAY
Miracles

ALSO BY LOUISE L. HAY

BOOKS/KITS

Colors & Numbers

Empowering Women

Everyday Positive Thinking

Experience Your Good Now!

A Garden of Thoughts: My Affirmation Journal

Gratitude: A Way of Life (Louise & Friends)

Heal Your Body

Heal Your Body A–Z

Heart Thoughts

I Can Do It® (book-with-CD)

Inner Wisdom

Letters to Louise

Life! Reflections on Your Journey

Love Your Body

Love Yourself, Heal Your Life Workbook

Meditations to Heal Your Life (also available in a gift edition)

The Power Is Within You

Power Thoughts

The Present Moment

The Times of Our Lives (Louise & Friends)

You Can Heal Your Life (also available in a gift edition)

You Can Heal Your Life Affirmation Kit

You Can Heal Your Life Companion Book

FOR CHILDREN

The Adventures of Lulu

I Think, I Am! (with Kristina Tracy)

Lulu and the Ant: A Message of Love

Lulu and the Dark: Conquering Fears

Lulu and Willy the Duck: Learning Mirror Work

CD PROGRAMS

Anger Releasing

Cancer

Change and Transition

Dissolving Barriers

Embracing Change

Feeling Fine Affirmations

Forgiveness/Loving the Inner Child

Heal Your Body (audio book)

How to Love Yourself

Life! Reflections on Your Journey (audio book)

Loving Yourself

Meditations for Personal Healing

Meditations to Heal Your Life (audio book)

Morning and Evening Meditations

101 Power Thoughts

Overcoming Fears

The Power Is Within You (audio book)

The Power of Your Spoken Word

Receiving Prosperity

Self-Esteem Affirmations
(subliminal)

Self-Healing

Stress-Free Affirmations
(subliminal)

Totality of Possibilities

What I Believe/Deep Relaxation

You Can Heal Your Life (audio book)

You Can Heal Your Life Study Course

Your Thoughts Create Your Life

DVDs

Dissolving Barriers

Embracing Change

You Can Heal Your Life Study Course

You Can Heal Your Life, The Movie (also available in an expanded edition)

CARD DECKS

Healthy Body Cards

I Can Do It® Cards

I Can Do It® Cards . . . for Creativity, Forgiveness, Health, Job Success, Wealth, Romance

Power Thought Cards

Power Thoughts for Teens

Power Thought Sticky Cards

Wisdom Cards

CALENDAR

I Can Do It® Calendar (for each individual year)

and

THE LOUISE L. HAY BOOK COLLECTION
(comprising the gift versions of *Meditations to Heal Your Life, You Can Heal Your Life,* and *You Can Heal Your Life Companion Book*)

All of the above are available at your local bookstore, or may be ordered by visiting:

Hay House USA: **www.hayhouse .com®**; Hay House Australia: **www .hayhouse.com.au;** Hay House UK: **www.hayhouse.co.uk;** Hay House South Africa: **www.hayhouse.co.za;** Hay House India: **www.hayhouse.co.in**

Louise's Websites: **www.LouiseHay .com®** and **www.HealYourLife.com®**

MODERN-DAY
Miracles

Miraculous Moments and Extraordinary Stories
from People All Over the World Whose Lives
Have Been Touched by Louise L. Hay

Louise L. Hay
& Friends

HAY HOUSE, INC.
Carlsbad, California • New York City
London • Sydney • Johannesburg
Vancouver • Hong Kong • New Delhi

Published and distributed in the United States by: Hay House, Inc.: www
.hayhouse.com • *Published and distributed in Australia by:* Hay House Australia
Pty. Ltd.: www.hayhouse.com.au • *Published and distributed in the United Kingdom by:* Hay House UK, Ltd.: www.hayhouse.co.uk • *Published and distributed in
the Republic of South Africa by:* Hay House SA (Pty), Ltd.: www.hayhouse.co.za •
Distributed in Canada by: Raincoast: www.raincoast.com • *Published in India
by:* Hay House Publishers India: www.hayhouse.co.in

Editorial supervision: Jill Kramer • *Project editor:* Shannon Littrell
Design: Riann Bender

Editor's note: All stories in this book have been Americanized and edited for
length and clarity, and only first names have been used. For those contributors
from the United States, we're listing their state; otherwise, we're listing the country
of origin. Certain exercises and affirmations have been excerpted from Louise's
books *Heart Thoughts, I Can Do It, The Power Is Within You, You Can Heal Your Life,*
and the *You Can Heal Your Life Companion Book,* all published by Hay House, Inc.

Library of Congress Cataloging-in-Publication Data

Modern-day miracles : miraculous moments and extraordinary stories from people all over the world whose lives have been touched by Louise L. Hay / Louise L.
Hay & friends. -- 1st ed.
      p. cm.
   ISBN 978-1-4019-2527-7 (tradepaper : alk. paper) 1. Conduct of life. 2. Spiritual life. 3. Hay, Louise L. I. Hay, Louise L.
   BJ1595.M66 2010
   158.092'2--dc22
                                    2010004593

ISBN: 978-1-4019-2527-7

13 12 11 10   4 3 2 1
1st edition, June 2010

Printed in the United States of America

I have long believed:

*"Everything I need to know
is revealed to me. Everything I need comes to me.
All is well in my life." There is no new knowledge.
All is ancient and infinite. It is my joy and pleasure
to gather together wisdom and knowledge for the
benefit of those on the healing pathway.*

*I dedicate this offering to all of you who have taught
me what I know: to my many clients, to my friends
in the field, to my teachers, and to the Divine
Infinite Intelligence for channeling through
me that which others need to hear.*

— Louise L. Hay

Contents

Introduction

by Louise L. Hay

Thirty years ago I wrote my first book, *Heal Your Body*, to help people recognize the importance of the mind-body connection. After enduring an abusive childhood spent in extreme poverty, as well as subsequent years of low self-esteem, I knew firsthand how influential replacing old negative beliefs with new and positive ones could be. And when I was later diagnosed with cancer, I understood that this was an opportunity to clear out my old patterns of resentment, once and for all. I did a lot of forgiveness work, released the pain of the past, and healed my body and spirit. Most important, I learned to genuinely love and approve of myself.

I then went on to write *You Can Heal Your Life*, incorporating all that I had learned into another book that could help others. Little did I know that these works would touch as many people as they have.

I started Hay House as a way to self-publish my books, and today, more than two decades later, I'm proud to say that we've grown to be one of the top publishers in the self-help/mind-body-spirit fields. I love supporting other authors who are helping people change their lives in meaningful ways.

Yet . . . I want to make it clear that *Modern-Day Miracles* is not intended to be an advertisement or endorsement for me or my company, nor is it meant to promote any particular spiritual path or viewpoint. What sparked this book is that my Hay House family and I have received countless letters over the years that have shared how I *inspired another person* to heal his or her own life (just as so many individuals have inspired *me* on my own healing journey). So, we thought it would be truly powerful and possibly life-changing to compile some of these amazing letters in one volume. Our hope is that they will provide you, the reader, with comfort, solace, and motivation—and point out in a concrete way that *one person* can be a catalyst for healing the world. I have been privileged to fulfill this role . . . and you can do it in your own life, too!

You'll notice that several universal topics are covered here, such as health, work, and love. Although many of the stories do have similar themes, they have been categorized based on the dominant issue facing the contributor. I introduce each chapter with a short paragraph; at the end of each chapter, there is a section in which I take you through some exercises to promote your own healing. (I suggest that you keep a notebook or journal nearby for this purpose.) I have also provided affirmations and a treatment that can work wonders on changing your consciousness in a positive way. Doing the work is a very important step in changing your life, as you will read in the following stories.

As you go through this book, which features contributions from people all over the world, please think about the ways in which *your* own thoughts, conversations, actions, and intentions can impact others in a positive way . . . because that's what life on this planet is all about. Lighting one candle in the darkness has the power to light another, and then another, and on and on it goes. . . .

Recently, I learned that my books have sold 50 million copies worldwide. I imagine 50 million candles lighting the way for another 50 million, and so on. How powerful each of our candles is! *Together, we can light up the entire world.*

Part I

Health and
Related Topics

Chapter One

Healing from Dis-ease

The word <u>disease</u> has too many of our old beliefs about health attached to it. I prefer to spell the word as <u>dis-ease</u> to signify those things that are not in harmony with us or our environment. This also empha-sizes that the natural state of the body is <u>ease.</u> I believe that every state of dis-ease is created by our thoughts. Our body wants good health and comfort. But our body is also listening to every word we think or speak about it, and reflecting our inner beliefs back to us. When we listen to our body instead of covering up every symptom with a pill, we under-stand what we require for healing. When we accept responsibility for our thoughts, we take back <u>control</u> of our health.

The people who have contributed the following stories demonstrate how listening to your body and changing your thoughts can create healing in all areas of your life.

Believe!
by Victoria, retired, California

"You have three months to live, maybe six," said the neurolo-gist to my husband of seven months. "I suggest you get your affairs in order." As we left the office, I felt numb. This could not be happening to us. We were still in the honeymoon phase, and I was determined to hold on to our joy and not lose Jim to brain cancer. We were not victims; we had the power to create miracles.

Although he knew when we married that I was interested in metaphysics, my new husband was not used to my way of looking at life. The son of a Marine Corps colonel, Jim grew up following the rules and conventional modes of thinking, and became a Marine himself. Now that he had been diagnosed with *glioblastoma multiforme,* one of the most lethal forms of brain cancer, he wanted to go the traditional route. This resulted in two brain surgeries, chemotherapy, and radiation. After following this program and learning that yet another tumor had grown during the process, he was now open to other methods, and we had no time to lose.

Jim and I agreed not to accept the reality that was painted by the medical community, but instead decided to create our own. The doctor was not God, and I knew that there were other possibilities in the universe for us. In order to bring in a healthy parallel reality, we pretended that he was *already* well. Even though he was incredibly weak and confined to a wheelchair, I asked my husband to remember how good it felt when he was at his physical peak, and we held steadfast to that feeling and vision. *Believe* became our mantra.

We continued to explore and incorporate ways to assist Jim's body in healing itself. Our course of action included everything we thought might work: taking mounds of supplements, juicing, toxin cleansing, acupuncture, and a clinic in Houston that for years was considered "alternative." We took measures to heal issues in present and past lives. People from all faiths prayed and imagined him as already well. We created a visualization technique that Jim repeated countless times in which the tumor shrank in size . . . and then it actually did disappear.

For those who witnessed our journey, my husband is considered a miracle. When anyone asks how he overcame the odds, the answer we give is simple, yet profound: *It's all in the mind.* Jim fought like a true warrior and won his greatest battle.

In my hands I hold the original "little blue book," *Heal Your Body,* by Louise Hay. Now yellowed and worn from 20 years of use, this book was the catalyst that brought me (and then my husband) a new way of understanding the relationship between the mind and body. The thoughts we think and the words we speak affect our bodies; by changing these patterns, we can all change the course of our lives. And so Jim and I did.

Ⱄ Ⱄ Ⱄ

Expect Miracles
by Barbara, elementary-school teacher, Canada

This past year I rediscovered Louise Hay through some of her audio programs, in addition to her beautiful DVD, *You Can Heal Your Life.* I was scheduled to have an operation because fluid had been found in my lungs, so the night before my surgery, I listened to one of Louise's evening meditations. The next morning, I woke up with one single thought: *Expect miracles.*

I was taken to the hospital, and before I knew it, I was in the recovery room with my husband at my side. I was informed that the surgeon had taken a look at my lungs prior to the procedure and seen that there was minimal fluid—he determined that I didn't need surgery, and I was cleared to go home. I was elated!

As I entered the front door and turned to head upstairs, I noticed a plaque on our wall that had been a gift from a friend. It read: EXPECT MIRACLES. I looked at my husband and said, "The power of positive thought and what we choose to focus our attention on really does come to fruition." After a giant bear hug, we continued our day, feeling relieved, blessed, and very grateful.

Thank you, Louise! With your help, I have overcome the fear of illness returning and instead focus each day on joy and healing. Your words continue to reach my subconscious, and today I'm back teaching part-time and passing on positive words of encouragement to my students.

Ⱄ Ⱄ Ⱄ

A Fire of Hope and Strength
by Alyssa, physician's assistant, Georgia

Having been diagnosed with an extremely rare and aggressive type of cancer at the age of 31, I was left both rocked by the shock of the news and gripped by an unshakable fear. The entire foundation of my life, which I'd stood so surely upon, seemed to disintegrate beneath me in an instant. Suddenly it felt as if I were falling into a dark abyss. As doctors attempted to figure out what was going on and what to do, I frantically tried to grasp how this had happened, as well as identify what this blur was that had become my life. As the reports came back one by one and the medical picture took form, things looked more and more bleak.

A darkness threatened to settle in, so I desperately searched for light. And I found it there on TV: in the form of a lovely, regal woman named Louise Hay. In her interview with Oprah Winfrey, Louise spoke powerful words of hope and kindness. She had the calm, reassuring voice of a loving mother; her tranquil confidence resonated somewhere deep within me. When all others talked only of dire statistics, poor outcomes, and grueling treatments, she dared to convey messages of healing and wholeness: "All is well." "Out of this experience, only good will come." "Everything is working out for my highest good." "I am safe." It was the speck of light I had been searching and hoping for. As I listened to Louise speak, it was as if the flame inside of me that had felt snuffed out was now reignited. I somehow knew that it could be fanned into a fire of hope and strength—I could rise from these ashes and then step forward into a healthy new life.

After the interview was over, I dove into using affirmations, claiming perfect wellness and permanent healing as my Divine Right. As I read more about Louise's vision of healing, wholeness, abundance, and love, it was as if a curtain had been pulled back. What was revealed was a beautiful mystery, a blueprint of an enigma decoded and of wisdom shared.

While my medical team did their work, I did mine. I began to untangle myself from old patterns and beliefs that had been keeping me from opening my heart and life to their true essence and potential. What doctors thought to be an extraordinary medical response, I knew were my affirmations and visualizations becoming reality. Then after my physical rebirth occurred, my spiritual one followed, sometimes even taking the lead. I began to see the rare opportunity I'd been given to "clean out" my life and choose what I wanted to put back in, to redefine everything. And what had started out as a desperate grab at hope became a clear path to awakening and healing.

Louise, you showed me the way home—you are truly a beacon of light, love, and hope for us all. I thank you with all my heart for rekindling the fire inside of me.

✗ ✗ ✗

Wandering My Way to Louise
by Debbie, business owner and retired teacher, Texas

In June 2007 I was diagnosed with a rare form of cancer, a gastro-intestinal stromal tumor. After surgery to remove the tumor, all but one of my doctors insisted that I needed further treatment, but chemo and radiation would not work. I admit that I was uneasy but not really scared. My feelings at the time were much more characterized by determination than fear. I knew I was going to do something to get well—I just wasn't sure what it was. I did make up my mind that whatever it was, it would be something that would not harm me in any way.

Since I was unsure of just what I needed to do, I went with my gut feelings and let myself become a wanderer. I wandered from room to room in my home. I wandered outside in my yard, constantly looking up to watch the clouds during the day and the stars at night. Even though it may have seemed that I was looking for something in all of these places, I knew I was actually searching for what I already had. I was confident that whatever it was would come to me at the perfect time.

One of my favorite places to go was a shopping area near my home. At one end is a Whole Foods Market, which became very instrumental in meeting my nutritional needs, and at the other end is a Barnes & Noble. About four or five weeks following my diagnosis, I found myself in this bookstore, wandering around. I remember looking up at a shelf and seeing a single copy of a book that had been pulled out. I felt a strong urge to reach up and take that volume off the shelf. When I saw its title, I actually started to laugh, thinking, *I wish. Wouldn't that be nice?* Yet I heeded the advice of my inner voice and purchased that book. Of course, it was *You Can Heal Your Life.*

When I returned home, I devoured Louise's book. As I read the words, I knew that this was what I'd been waiting to discover. I immediately started doing the affirmations, exercises, and visualizations Louise suggested; the more I practiced, the better I got at doing them.

It's now been a year and a half, and I'm in excellent health! I have lots of energy and know that I'm living life the way I'm meant to—happy, fit, and vibrant! *You Can Heal Your Life* has become an inspirational guide that I continue to use. I will be eternally grateful to Louise.

❦ ❦ ❦

Modern Miracles Do Happen!
by Alana, yoga therapist and Reiki master, California

Louise Hay has been such an inspiration to me and has truly changed my life in the most positive way. When I needed a miracle, I listened to her every day from my sickbed, and the miracle came!

I was diagnosed with severe Crohn's disease in 2003. I went on to spend two years completely bedridden, in excruciating pain every day. I was on government disability, and after trying every medication and not having any of them work, the medical profession gave up on me. Doctors said it was highly unlikely that I'd ever get out of bed again.

My mother, who is a retired psychologist, never gave up hope that I'd someday get better. Louise Hay had helped my mom dramatically when she was going through a divorce; now, she brought me two of Louise's CDs so that we could listen to them together. I loved listening to these CDs—Louise's soothing voice entered my bedroom every day and made me feel so much better. It was as if she were my angel. I went on to read her books and say affirmations many times a day, which made a big difference in my life.

Modern miracles do happen! Every single day, I continued to work on my affirmations and positive thinking, and I slowly got healthier and healthier with time. Not only did I get out of bed, but I began to take classes in yoga and Reiki, which helped bring me to a state of true wellness. I can happily say that I'm now a yoga instructor, yoga therapist, and Reiki master. It is my goal to spread the work that so miraculously gave me my health back, so I specialize in working with people who have chronic or serious illness. I want to give back!

I begin every one of my yoga classes by allowing my students to pick a Louise Hay affirmation card; at the end of class, I invite them to take their card home and put it up somewhere. They love this! So many of my students have had positive experiences from just taking home one of these affirmation cards. My dream is to one day be able to help as many people as Louise has and to be able to give lectures and write books of encouragement and support myself. In 2007, I had the pleasure of attending the *I Can Do It!*® Conference in Las Vegas with my mother. It was one of the best trips I have ever been on, and it will always be a memory that I treasure and keep in my heart.

Louise, you were there when the medical profession gave up on me, and your gentle voice nurtured me back to health. For this, I am eternally grateful. To me, you are a miracle worker!

✘ ✘ ✘

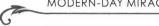

The Light of Health
by Alena, business owner and CEO, Canada

I come from a small country in the middle of Europe. In 1993 I first read one of Louise Hay's books, and for the first time in my life I felt like somebody was talking from my own heart. I didn't understand why I found her so late, at the age of 27. Now I know why: when a pupil is ready, a mentor appears.

Louise helped all aspects of my life, and then I went on to find Shakti Gawain, Napoleon Hill, Dale Carnegie, Norman Vincent Peale, and Stephen R. Covey. I learned a great deal from all of these wonderful writers, but Louise remains my favorite.

The way in which Louise has really affected my life is in the area of health. When I first discovered her, I'd been suffering from streptococcal tonsillitis (ST) very often every year, for 22 years. Several doctors confirmed this diagnosis, although none of them ever did a lab test. They were absolutely certain it was ST and always prescribed antibiotics. Sometimes I'd have a series of ST infections, one after another, for six weeks in a row—and this meant that every second or third week I'd be given antibiotics, one after another.

It was Louise's teachings and my husband's great support that gave me the encouragement to turn things around. So, the next time I was diagnosed with ST and given a course of antibiotics, I decided to get rid of the disease without taking one single pill. And I did just that!

I meditated with the affirmations Louise shared in her book *You Can Heal Your Life* and followed her other advice, including eating a light diet to get rid of toxins and letting my body do its job and heal itself. Seven days later, I went to my doctor for a follow-up. When she confirmed that I was completely healthy, I almost fainted, that's how excited I was to hear the news. My miracle is that I was healed without antibiotics, and to this very day, I've never had ST again.

Louise, you've been there from the very beginning of my great journey, and I have learned so much because of you. Thanks to you, I found the light at the end of the tunnel—and thanks to you again, I'm now living in this light. I am so grateful, Louise, and I have so much love and respect for you. Be proud of yourself.

✘ ✘ ✘

The Mind's Healing Power
by B. J., retired, Texas

After suffering months of thoracic pain in the early months of 2004, I visited three different doctors and was put through many tests, yet no one could find the source of my pain. That June, I was getting out of the car when I fell to the ground, paralyzed from just above the waist on down. Fortunately, a friend was with me and called for an ambulance. At the hospital, an MRI showed a massive tumor on my upper spine, which had metastasized from breast cancer. I was told that I needed surgery immediately to remove the tumor and make me comfortable until the end, which would be just four to five months away, although my daughter was told that I wouldn't survive the surgery itself.

The next day, my 63rd birthday, the tumor was removed. I was in the intensive care unit (ICU) for 48 hours. When I'd survived that long, I was moved to a private room. The doctors were amazed, but they assured me that I wouldn't walk again. I had several weeks of radiation on my spine and began drug therapy for the breast cancer. The doctors were again amazed when I began to wiggle one big toe, but they promised me that was as good as it would get.

After being transferred to a rehab facility, I had another near-death experience as blood clots entered my lungs. Again, I was rushed by ambulance to a nearby hospital and placed in the ICU; once again, my daughter was told this was the end. I contracted a staph infection from the insertion of a filter to prevent more blood clots from entering my lungs or heart, but I was transferred back to rehab after four weeks. There, I spent the next six weeks in physical and occupational therapy. One of the technicians insisted that I could walk and would not take no for an answer. At first I only took a few halting steps, but when I left rehab, I could walk around the gym with assistance and a walker.

After being in four different hospitals in four months, I spent the next eight months with my daughter and her family and continued to recover. It took a while, but I'm again living alone, driving, and doing most of the things I want to do. I've been cancer free for three years, and although my walking is not as it used to be, I *can* walk—and without a cane or other assistance.

You may wonder where Louise Hay fits in to all of this. Well, during my early hospital days, my daughter brought me books and CDs, and I found Louise's to be especially helpful. I played her CDs continually; when I wasn't listening to them, I was meditating and repeating affirmations. I wouldn't be walking or healed or even alive today had it not been for Louise's words. I realized that the illness was in my mind, and there it could be healed. Louise reminded me to change my thoughts and thus change my life. I continue to enjoy her products and am so grateful to her.

❦ ❦ ❦

Embracing Multiple Sclerosis
by Victoria, graphic designer, Canada

I was diagnosed with "relapsing-remitting multiple sclerosis" in 1987. My symptoms were blurred vision and numbness in my hands, arms, and legs. My neurologist told me that there wasn't any medication available for me at this point and I'd be in a wheelchair in two years. *No I won't,* I thought.

I decided to "speak" to my multiple sclerosis (MS). I told it that I would respect it; in return, it would have to respect *me* and let me live my life. When I didn't respect *myself,* I'd have attacks of blurred vision and weakness in my arms and legs that would last for two or three months. This went on for 15 years, until my disease became aggravated because of personal issues in 2003.

At this point, the disease accelerated into "secondary progressive multiple sclerosis." I had no balance and, according to the doctors, no chance for a remission. I could no longer walk without the assistance of a walker. I was in excruciating pain, which felt like electric shocks traveling through my head and shoulders. My speech was slurred, I was choking on my food, I had no coordination in my limbs, and I was sleeping all the time. My symptoms were a reflection of what was going on in my mind, which was overwhelmed by the controlling emotions of resentment, anger, and fear.

By this time, I'd discovered Louise Hay, whose teachings showed me that I had to take responsibility for my own disease. I was the only one who could decide if I would ever walk again, and I had to be able to stand up for myself. MS was not a terrible diagnosis but a blessing in disguise. My body was speaking to me and telling me that I was able to walk on my own if I so chose. To do so, I had to be more independent and make my own decisions.

I began to say affirmations on a daily basis, truly feeling them, and I started turning my life around. I moved away from fear and made my decisions based on love and truth. By loving myself, honoring my body, and not treating myself as a victim, I created the most extraordinary version of myself. I also started to attract like-minded, positive, and supportive people into my life.

I've been doing Pilates and taking belly-dancing lessons. I have started art classes and am continuing my career as a graphic designer. I am now able to speak and see clearly, I have more energy, and my coordination has improved 100 percent. I view my walker as a support, not as a crutch. Reading Louise's books and saying her affirmations daily—and, most important, feeling them in my heart—have made me embrace MS and given me the inner peace to move forward fearlessly. I am now the woman I was born to be, and I am confident in my abilities!

✉ ✉ ✉

Louise Inspires and Helps Heal
by Mary, musician, artist, and writer, California

Louise Hay has been an inspiration to me since 1986. I was living in San Francisco at the time, and one day while perusing the shelves of a local bookstore, a copy of *You Can Heal Your Life* seemed to fall right into my hands. Of course, I bought it . . . and I still have this dog-eared copy and refer to it often.

I identified with Louise right away: I'm single; I was raised in Christian Science, but it wasn't really to my liking; and in 1983, I began practicing Transcendental Meditation and studying New Thought soon after. I've gone on to purchase so many of Louise's products over the years that Hay House gifted me with a white leather-bound version of *You Can Heal Your Life*. It is one of my treasures.

I've experienced so much inspiration and enlightenment from Louise's work through the years. For example, in February 1988, after sensing that something was seriously wrong with me, I received two diagnoses of a cervical-cancer condition. I hardly told anyone about this and simply decided to head to the Optimum Health Institute (OHI), a place I know that Louise also loves, in San Diego. I drove down from the Mendocino coast, where I'd moved a few months before to indulge my burning desire to play jazz piano, and spent two weeks "taking the cure." The real healing balm was an early audio-cassette of Louise's counsel and affirmations (a kind friend made the tape for me and I don't even know its title). Louise's soothing voice helped me relax into OHI's regimen, and I've always felt that absorbing the truth of her words was a major part of my healing.

I knew I was well when I left OHI, but several months later I went to a traditional medical doctor for a checkup. I was pronounced healthy, completely clean and clear of the condition, and I have remained so ever since.

Thank you for giving me the opportunity to share this story, Louise. I send you much love!

⚸ ⚸ ⚸

Bringing My "Stuff" to the Surface
by Renee, Somato Respiratory Integration (SRI)
facilitator, New York

Ten years ago I was in the hospital to give birth to my second daughter. The day after I had her, I discovered a golf-ball-sized lump on my neck. Long story short, it was a cancerous tumor on my thyroid; doctors wanted to operate and start chemotherapy and radiation right away. Thankfully, I said, "No, I want to take my baby home."

In complete shock, I prayed to everything, even my plants, for answers. I went to the bookstore to learn about my options, because surgery was not one of them for me (I didn't want to stop breast-feeding my baby). Louise Hay's book *You Can Heal Your Life* caught my eye and sang to my soul. Thanks to that book, I went on to spend countless hours with affirmations and deep breathing, and I cried lots of tears. My "stuff" came to the surface to be examined and then healed . . . including the rheumatoid arthritis that I've had since I was three. Needless to say, I was up to my eyeballs in issues from my past, but some things have to get worse before they get better!

I'm pleased to tell you that I healed myself, without any drugs or operations, and I couldn't have done it without Louise Hay. I tell everyone that if I were stranded on an island, *You Can Heal Your Life* is the book I would want to have with me. Someday I will look Louise in the eyes and try to give back all that she's given me. My heart is filled with many blessings for this remarkable woman.

∦ ∦ ∦

Defying All Medical History
by Sue, sales manager, Texas

I am whole in body, mind, and spirit . . . <u>all</u> is well in my world!
That statement from Louise Hay has been my mantra and my "lifeline" since 1999, always embedded in my mind and taped to

my bathroom mirror. On August 31 of that year, I was diagnosed with multiple myeloma. I was told that it wasn't curable, but it *was* treatable and controllable. I made the choice that this would not be my reality! The week after I was diagnosed, a friend bought me *You Can Heal Your Life* on tape. I listened to it religiously, and within a few weeks, Louise's eloquent yet profoundly powerful message resonated in a place deep within me. I knew I was going to live because I believed that *I am whole in body, mind, and spirit . . . all is well in my world!*

Over my journey in the years that followed, I continued to recite that statement. The book version of *You Can Heal Your Life* has become my guide for living; and *Heal Your Body, 101 Ways to Health and Healing,* and the *Power Thought Cards* are always on my nightstand or by my side!

It is abundantly clear to me that Louise's positive affirmations and inspiration empowered me to live. And my miracle was confirmed on July 9, 2008, when my oncologist told me, "Sue, I can't believe I'm saying this because it defies all medical history, but you are cured, free of myeloma—it's gone! You are truly a walking miracle!" I know in my heart that my never-ending faith in God, and my positive attitude thanks to always having Louise Hay with me, are the reasons why I am a very happy and healthy woman today.

I am forever indebted to you, Louise, for your constant desire to help people like me. *Thank you!*

↯ ↯ ↯

I've Manifested a Glorious Life!
by Iwona, photographer, United Kingdom

Regular outbreaks of genital herpes had been bothering me for about two years. They took place every couple of months, and I treated every single one of them with a trip to the hospital and a packet of antibiotics. It would then take another week or so for the outbreak to heal.

One day, noting the usual discomfort that preceded an out-break, I decided to apply the philosophy of Louise Hay. I'd been reading her books for a number of years, and I knew that I couldn't be on antibiotics and accept the idea of my mind being able to heal and manifest at the same time.

I realized that my job was now to go as deep as I could into my old patterns of rejecting my own sexual organs as a young adult . . . so that's what I did. I recalled the times when I believed my genitals were ugly and embarrassing, when I couldn't touch them or even look at them. I never used tampons during my period because I couldn't conceive of having something in my vagina. And, of course, I couldn't even imagine having sex. All this eased a little bit when I turned 20 and felt that it was time to "grow up." Even so, I was now realizing how I'd created very regular herpes outbreaks that began to show up a few years later.

I started my inner work on those negative patterns with great hope and a joyous feeling of just overcoming them. I wouldn't mention the word *pain* to myself, deliberately replacing it with *sensation,* so I wouldn't give power to the illusion of disease. I used the affirmation for herpes from Louise's book *You Can Heal Your Life* and adopted it as my mantra. I'd repeat it over and over, with the deep belief that I was already healed. I visualized my sexual organs as healthy, glowing with their natural beauty, as often as I could. I did my best to create the atmosphere of wellness and appreciation for my beautiful genitals, and I did feel like I was healing very fast.

After four days of my work, I had an amazing dream. In it, I went to the hospital to see if my herpes was gone, even though I intuitively knew I'd been healed. The doctor did an examination and said, "I can see the effect of Louise's affirmations and your other mental work here. Everything looks fine, and you are completely healed."

I woke up with a tingling feeling that a huge miracle had just occurred. My dream assured me that I'd been healed, and I'd done it with the power of my mind and no antibiotics! This experience gave me a very strong belief in doing mental work and going within to create the outer world. Everybody has the potential to manifest glorious lifetimes filled with love and magic.

It is years later, and I haven't had a single outbreak. I am truly healed, thanks to Louise!

⚞ ⚟ ⚞

Love Heals

by Jodie Kristine, vice president of a
residential-appraisal company, California

I was diagnosed with Crohn's disease in 1987 at the age of 24. Even as I took my medications, I suffered terribly. By 1989 my health had deteriorated to the point that my doctor said he was going to put me on steroids and might need to perform a surgery in which he'd remove part of my intestines. I was so sick and tired of being sick and tired—yet I knew that I didn't want surgery, since it would just be a Band-Aid that wouldn't accomplish any real healing. I needed to find a cure, so I started praying.

A friend invited me to a performance at the Circle Star Theater in San Carlos, California, and that's where I met Louise Hay. My life changed from that point on . . . I found out that love heals. I started doing my affirmations daily in the mirror, constantly repeating: *I accept and approve of myself.* Today, I am a miracle: at age 45, I take no medication, and I'm in better shape than I was 20 years ago. I get a colonoscopy every two years, and each test has shown continued healing in my intestinal walls.

Thank you, Louise, for being you and sharing your knowledge so that I could heal my life. I have a picture of you on my desk at home, and it reminds me to do my work and give thanks to you. My husband and I recently saw you in Los Angeles—what a joy it was to talk to you again after all these years. I send you love and blessings.

⚞ ⚟ ⚞

My Miraculous Path

by Gayle, registered nurse, licensed massage therapist,
macrobiotic educator, and personal chef, Florida

In 1970, I was a 14-year-old free spirit. The world was beautiful, as it was the age of peace and love, the dawning of Aquarius. I became a vegetarian and a yogi, and I lived blissfully along this path.

I finished college in 1978, and auspiciously found an apartment at a yoga center after graduation. The woman who ran the center became the unconditionally loving mother I'd always longed for. I called her "Swami Mommy," and she was everything to me. I would have stayed with her forever, but life moved me away. My interest in nutrition led me to nursing school, and I became fully immersed in the medical world. Day after day, I witnessed surgery, medication, sickness like no one should ever have to see, and death. I totally fell off the path!

A relentless desire to return to my yoga teacher's side finally brought me back to her in 1994. I was happy to see that her yoga center was flourishing; I remembered my youth and was blissfully back on the path. Then on November 9, 1996, my Swami Mommy suddenly died. The love and nurturing she gave me was gone, and it felt as if my heart had exploded. I had terrible pain in my back, and it was like everything in my body broke. Just a short time later, I found a lump in my breast. It turns out that I had breast cancer, and it had spread into 12 lymph nodes. Medically, I received a death sentence—I was told that I had six months to one year to live.

But my Swami Mommy had left me a gift: a yoga student of hers who lived in a tent at the center. This wonderful man had few possessions, but he did have a beat-up paperback book called *Heal Your Body*, by Louise L. Hay. "You have to read this," he said. So I did.

I have heard that a teacher can touch you, that his or her words can resonate with you, and that healing can take place instantly. I think it did for me the day I opened that book. *My back. My breast. Cancer.* Louise provided the cause for every one of the problems I was having. I recited the affirmations she provided. I absorbed her own story about healing from cancer. And I believed that *I* could heal, too.

I have seen colorful, shiny, brand-new copies of many of Louise Hay's books ever since that day in 1996 when that wonderful man (who went on to become my husband) shared *Heal Your Body* with me. But I will never part with the tattered, taped-together copy that we still use all the time.

It is now 2009, and I am alive and vibrantly healthy. I thank Louise Hay every day for writing the book that taught me how to heal my body.

This is my miracle.

※ ※ ※

The Magical Book
by Maria Isabel, sales executive, Ecuador

In May 2006 I was diagnosed with breast cancer. It was a very hard time, and I didn't know what to do. My sister-in-law brought me the book *The Power Is Within You,* written by Louise Hay, and it just seemed magical to me. As I started my treatment, I remembered what I'd read, and I practiced everything that Louise said. I completed the treatment without any problems—everything was right, and my recovery was easy. I know that most people with cancer wouldn't say that the experience was an opportunity to get to something incredible and discover all the opportunities that one has in life. But that's the attitude I had, and everything turned out wonderfully.

At the time I started the treatment, I also started to rebuild my house and continued with my work (I work on a flower farm, one hour from my town). I continued doing normal things and didn't change my life. I was sure that everything would go the right way, I'd be healthy, and my whole life would be terrific . . . and I was right! I now have more opportunities than I had before, and I'm sure that I'm going to have a long, happy life. Yes!

I'm sure that God put Louise Hay's book in my hands, and I am so grateful to Him (and her!).

⚡ ⚡ ⚡

Totally Healed in Every Way

by Jaimi, massage therapist, California

Over the spring and summer of 2006, I had a flare-up of my ulcerative colitis. I'd seen a few doctors, but they never did anything to help. So I spent May through July hidden inside my house, fearful of leaving in case I wouldn't make it to the nearest bathroom in time—unfortunately, this had happened to me in the past, and I totally embarrassed myself. I was a slave to the toilet. I never knew when an episode would occur, but when it did, I could be incapacitated for hours on end. Sometimes I'd lie on my bed in such excruciating pain that I wished I could just die and be done with it. My kids became very independent, which I guess was a good thing now that I think about it, but at the time caused me to feel completely helpless.

One day I did leave the house for a few minutes to walk my dogs, and a neighbor told me about Louise Hay and her book *You Can Heal Your Life*. She told me that the ideas Louise presented in those pages might be tough for me, but if I was willing to do the work, I'd be healed. Since I've always considered myself a spiritual person, I believed that I was up for the challenge.

Since finishing *You Can Heal Your Life* and doing its exercises a few years ago, I can say that I am totally healed. Yes, it has been an arduous road, but it's one that I would take again and again. My life, and my views about my life, has completely changed. And I've continued on my journey: I've seen spiritual therapists, acupuncturists, and shamans; and I've read books by Doreen Virtue, Brandon Bays, and other spiritual writers.

I am so grateful for all I have learned about myself, and am still learning. Not only have I changed my own life, but the process has also helped the people around me. I am a better person today, and I thank God and the Universe for having had this experience. I appreciate everything, everyone, and every day. I have so much gratitude for the universe, but I give a *big* thanks to Louise Hay and bless her every single day! She is my guru. I believe that she is the reason I am where I am today: healed, healthy, grateful, and happy!

Thank you, Louise, from the bottom of my heart—and my healthy colon!

꒰ ꒰ ꒰

Free of Cancer and Full of Blessings
by Lin, literacy coach, New Jersey

It is only a thought, and a thought can be changed. This became my chant more than 15 years ago when I discovered that I had breast cancer.

While writing my thesis on the mind-body connection, I found a store that sold Louise Hay's work, and I was drawn to the book and audio program of *You Can Heal Your Life*. Miracles were instantly set in motion, and so many things fell into place as I needed them.

Cancer turns your world upside down. So even though it was winter and cold, I'd walk and walk with my husband to release my negative energy. After we came home, I'd put on Louise's tape to fall asleep. Whenever I became upset, I'd focus on changing my negative thoughts. And I kept saying my affirmation over and over.

A doctor who specialized in breast cancer was soon recommended to me by several people. I called my insurance company to request that he treat me, and I was told that the agreement was just now being signed to have him become a participating doctor in my health plan. I finally felt that I was in the right place to successfully treat my cancer. I found other positive-thinking authors like Bernie Siegel, and resources such as *A Course in Miracles,* so I was well on my way to healing.

I'm now cancer free and grateful for the groundwork Louise Hay laid for me. So many doors have been opened for me in life, and I've been truly blessed. It is a beautiful thing!

❦ ❦ ❦

Smiles and Miracles
by Nancy, job not supplied, Nevada

My life challenges began in the womb. I was such a sad, shame-ridden little girl that by the age of 13, I still didn't know how to smile. I'd read in a magazine that it was a good idea to smile at the people you pass each day, so I went to the bathroom mirror to see how that would look. When I made the attempt, what I felt was pain in the muscles of my face; what I saw in the mirror was an unpleasant grimace. Shocked, I was determined to replace this with a model's smile. I practiced for months before I had the courage to try it out in public. When I did, an elderly man kindly returned my smile. I was stunned. This proved to be a life-changing event.

Another life-changing event occurred when I was 52 and diagnosed with breast cancer. I was scheduled to have a large part of my right breast removed, followed by chemotherapy, just like my own mother had done (she'd died of breast cancer at age 54). On the day I was to have the surgery, I woke up and called the doctor's office, telling them that I wouldn't be having it done. Surprisingly, the nurse who'd answered the phone replied, "Good for you!"

I had no idea what to do or how I was going to go about curing the cancer—but the Universe did. I was led to one person after another who enlightened me as to alternative healing methods. Then Louise Hay's book *You Can Heal Your Life* came to me. Naturally, I was thrilled to read how she'd been healed of cancer. I began applying her teachings, along with the others things I'd learned. I went on to heal myself, and I've had normal mammograms for the past seven years.

Recently, I came upon Louise at the *I Can Do It!* Conference in Las Vegas. I shared the impact of her book's teachings, which I'd continued to learn from. I told her how I taught my grown children the principles I'd learned from her and the outstanding results they continue to experience—my eldest son even asks for her *I Can Do It* calendar every year for Christmas.

Not all miracles are earthshaking, newsworthy events. Often, they're tiny seeds of good planted by those who are willing to share them. These seeds that struggle in the storms of life then grow into strong examples that inspire and encourage others along life's path.

As Louise and I spoke that day, she took my hands in hers and asked, "Do you know how powerful you are?" I hesitated slightly. Then I saw the journey I'd embarked on, from a 13-year-old child who couldn't even smile to a mature woman who said "No!" to breast cancer, one who continues to plant Louise Hay's miraculous seeds of good.

I looked Louise boldly in the eyes, smiled broadly, and emphatically said, "Yes, I do!"

Doing the Work with Louise

When treating any medical issue, it's important to talk to a health-care professional. However, it's also important to discover the root of the illness within you. You cannot completely cure a dis-ease by only treating the physical symptoms. Your body will continue to manifest illness until you heal the emotional and spiritual issues that are the source of the dis-ease.

You will get a better understanding of your thoughts about health by completing the exercises below. (Please write your answers on a separate piece of paper or in your journal.)

Releasing Your Health Problems

True healing involves body, mind, and spirit. I believe that if we "cure" an illness yet do not address the emotional and spiritual issues that surround that ailment, it will only manifest again.

So, are you willing to release the need that has contributed to your health problems? Keep in mind that when you have a condition that you want to change, the first thing you have to do is say so. Say, *"I am willing to release the need in me that has created this condition."* Say it again. Say it looking in the mirror. Say it every time you think about your condition. It's the first step to creating change.

The Role of Illness in Your Life

Next, complete the following statements as honestly as you can:

1. *The way I make myself sick is . . .*
2. *I get sick when I try to avoid . . .*
3. *When I get sick, I always want to . . .*
4. *When I was sick as a child, my mother/father always . . .*
5. *My greatest fear when I'm sick is that . . .*

Your Family History

Then take a moment to do the following:

1. List all of your mother's illnesses.
2. List all of your father's illnesses.
3. List all of your illnesses.
4. Do you see a connection?

Your Beliefs about Dis-ease

Let's take a closer look at your beliefs about dis-ease. Answer the following questions:

1. What do you remember about your childhood illnesses?

2. What did you learn from your parents about dis-ease?

3. What, if anything, did you enjoy about being sick as a child?

4. Is there a belief about illness from your childhood that you're still acting on today?

5. How have you contributed to the state of your health?

6. Would you like your health to change? If so, in what way?

Self-Worth and Health

Now let's examine the issue of self-worth with respect to your health. Answer the following questions. After each one, say one or more of the positive affirmations that follow to counteract the negative belief.

1. Do you feel you deserve good health?
2. What do you fear most about your health?
3. What are you "getting" from this belief?
4. What do you fear will happen if you let go of this belief?

Affirmations

Every day I feel better and better.

I am beautiful and empowered at any age.

I am feeling wonderfully well. I radiate good health.

My body heals rapidly.

I am filled with energy and enthusiasm.

My loving thoughts keep my immune system strong.
    I am safe inside and out.

I am healthy and whole and filled with joy.

I have a happy, agile body.

I am willing to release the pattern in my consciousness
    that has created this condition.

I appreciate the wonder of my body.

I love myself and am gentle with my body.

I maintain my body at optimal health.

I love life. It is safe for me to live.

I am healthy, whole, and complete.

I go within to dissolve the pattern that created this.
    I now accept Divine healing.

I am totally comfortable at all times.

Every hand that touches me in a medical setting is
    a healing hand and expresses only love.

My surgery goes quickly and easily and perfectly.

With every breath I take, I am getting healthier
    and healthier.

Good health is mine now. I release the past.

Treatment for Dis-ease

I accept health as the natural state of my being. I now consciously release any mental patterns within me that could express as dis-ease in any way. I love and approve of myself. I love and approve of my body. I feed it nourishing foods and beverages. I exercise it in ways that are fun. I recognize my body as a wondrous and magnificent machine, and I feel privileged to live in it. I love having lots of energy.
All is well in my world.

Chapter Two

Dealing with Injury and Pain

Pain comes in so many different forms. Often people try to hide from it, hoping that it will go away or that they can cover it up with medication. But ignoring your body just makes it try harder to get your attention—your body is asking for your help.

In order to heal the thoughts and beliefs that are the true source of your pain, you must face that pain head-on. One way to deal with it is to change your perception of the situation; simply do not give in to it! For example, instead of focusing on the fact that your wrist hurts, try referring to your wrist as having a lot of <u>sensation.</u> This can help you get through the unpleasant experience and allow you to focus on healing your mind and soul. Healing the pain will then follow.

I hope you find inspiration in the following stories of recovery.

A Broken Body and a Rebuilt Life
by Martez, registered massage and
craniosacral therapist, Canada

In 1987, while vacationing in Florida, I was involved in a severe motor-vehicle accident, and my life changed in an instant. The head-on collision left me with much of my body injured: I had a

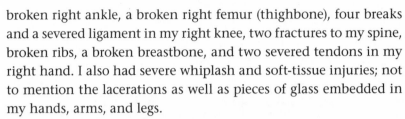

broken right ankle, a broken right femur (thighbone), four breaks and a severed ligament in my right knee, two fractures to my spine, broken ribs, a broken breastbone, and two severed tendons in my right hand. I also had severe whiplash and soft-tissue injuries; not to mention the lacerations as well as pieces of glass embedded in my hands, arms, and legs.

Up until that time, I was a very active, independent 24-year-old working as a clothing designer. I knew very little about the body, other than how to create clothing for it. For the most part, I was living my life pretty unconsciously, feeling that I wasn't on my true path. Now here I was in the hospital, preparing to have the first of seven surgeries that would take place over the next four years.

Just prior to the accident, I was given a few books—one of which was Louise Hay's "little blue book," *Heal Your Body.* As I recovered from my injuries, I soaked up what was in those pages and learned how changing my thoughts could change my life. I knew that on the long road of recovery that was ahead of me, my thoughts, be they positive or negative, would impact how that recovery went. I read about the power of affirmations and began saying them right there in the hospital; over and over, I'd repeat: *Every day in every way, I am getting better and better, stronger, and healthier.*

In two weeks I left the hospital with a full leg cast and an arm cast, and I needed a wheelchair. I eventually graduated from forearm crutches to a cane, but then I endured years of appointments with doctors, specialists, and therapists . . . and their prognoses weren't optimistic.

My affirmations helped me cope with the sudden changes to my body, mind, and spirit—not to mention my life—and helped me stay focused on where I was headed. There was one procedure in particular that I was nervous about, which would be a double surgery on the front and back of my hand. Right up until I had the anesthetic, I repeated this affirmation: *I am recovering quickly and easily with very little pain.* And that's exactly what happened! Although it was one of the most complicated surgeries I went through, I had very little pain and recovered very quickly.

I continued to heal from the accident, and today I'm doing extremely well. As a result of all my experiences, I decided to go back to school and became a registered massage and craniosacral therapist. I incorporate affirmations in my work and help educate my clients on how their thoughts affect their lives and health. I've now been practicing for 16 years.

Thank you, Louise! I'm forever grateful to you.

✗ ✗ ✗

Healing Begins by Loving Yourself
by Anne, holistic-fitness practitioner, Nevada

By most people's standards, the last several years of my life have been a medical nightmare. But I view them as a journey of healing that led me to discover my purpose in life.

It began in 1992, when an ectopic pregnancy made it necessary for me to undergo surgery to remove my right fallopian tube. Two years later, I had another surgery: a laparoscopy to assess whether I'd become infertile. Unfortunately, this procedure caused an obstruction in my small intestine, and I was rushed to the emergency room for my third surgery. I had a bowel resection, during which the doctor removed two and a half feet of my small intestine, cauterized the bowel, and cut away scar tissue from my fallopian tubes. I was in the ICU for three weeks, and I nearly died.

When I finally left the hospital, I weighed 80 pounds. My intestine hadn't healed properly, so I was unable to digest food. In addition, I experienced painful menstrual cramps and heavy bleeding, chronic diarrhea, and anemia. My bones were sticking out of my body, and my hair was falling out. Bedridden, I felt weak, alone, scared, and depressed. This went on for two years.

The doctors said that my chances of having children were gone; on top of that, they weren't able to treat me any longer. I was devastated. Yet in the midst of this pain and confusion, I came across Louise Hay's book *You Can Heal Your Life.* As I read it, I no longer felt helpless and alone. I read Louise's affirmations daily, and they helped me through endless nights of pain. Her message was clear: *If you're willing to do the work, anything can be healed—and healing begins by loving yourself.*

Inspired by what I read in *You Can Heal Your Life,* I made a conscious decision at the age of 32 to take ownership of my health. I began a program of alternative healing with acupuncture and herbs and entered a holistic-healing center, where they incorporated yoga, tai chi, Qi gong, meditation, visualization, and energy-healing sessions from a master healer. Thanks to positive thinking, exercise, and a specific diet, my symptoms disappeared in just over two months. I also became pregnant again. Even though I had another ectopic pregnancy, this demonstrated to me that my body had healed from all the work I had done. It was a miracle that I was able to become pregnant at all.

I became certified as an energy healer and holistic-fitness instructor in Sedona, Arizona, where I fell in love with my spiritual partner, Mitch. We got married and ended up adopting a beautiful baby girl, Arianna. She is my gift from God.

I reference Louise Hay's guidebook, *Heal Your Body,* and use her affirmations on a daily basis in all my classes. I can testify to the truth of Louise's teachings: that you can heal yourself of any health condition by loving yourself and releasing your limiting beliefs from your past.

ᴋ ᴋ ᴋ

Dancing Like a New Person
by Shira, student, Israel

A few years ago I decided to follow my dream and study dance. The first year that I spent at a professional school was so amazing to me—I started my day with a ballet class every morning, and in the afternoon I was in the studio, dancing and strengthening my body from class to class.

Before the second year of school, I began to feel pain in my lower back. When the pain kept growing and increasing in intensity, I went to the doctor. An x-ray showed that I had a herniated disk, which was quite shocking to me. I read all about it on the Internet, and I found out that this condition isn't something you can heal from; it stays with you forever. You can cut it away with surgery, but one sure thing is that you'll suffer from pain all your life. This news was like an earthquake for me. The realization that I'd never be able to dance again made me incredibly sad.

When it was time to return to school, I tried to participate in classes, but I just couldn't. I sat in the corner of the studio, thinking, *Why is this happening to me?* I was being treated by a special doctor who gave me massages, but that wasn't very helpful. I walked around like a ghost, until my friend Adva took me aside for a serious talk. She brought me Louise Hay's book *You Can Heal Your Life* and made me promise to read it.

I took a week to stay home and read Louise's book and practice her exercises. The first time I had to stand in front of the mirror and tell myself how much I loved myself, I couldn't do it. Every time I had to tell myself that I was willing to let go of whatever had brought me to this situation, I cried. But I continued to do what Louise suggested. I was aware of my thoughts all the time; I started writing positive letters to myself; I told myself how much I loved myself 300 times a day; I meditated; I tried to forgive; and slowly but surely, I started to smile again.

A short time after going through the process in *You Can Heal Your Life*, my doctor said that he thought it was time to work with me in a different way than before. Like magic, just a week later, I couldn't feel the pain anymore. I came back to the studio and danced like a new person, because I knew I'd healed myself!

Thank you, Louise!

❦ ❦ ❦

My Own Best Healer
by Dionne, interior designer, California

I discovered Louise Hay in 1994. I read *You Can Heal Your Life* cover to cover several times, since the ideas presented in those pages were revolutionary to me. Although I'd heard of the mind-body connection before, the idea that I could change my thoughts and then change my health thrilled me.

At the time, I was suffering from extremely painful carpal tunnel syndrome in my right wrist, which was interfering with my life on a daily basis. Knowing that surgery produced iffy results for many people, I decided that I had nothing to lose by trying Louise's affirmations. I repeated them hundreds of times daily, whenever I had a quiet space and could remember to do so. Within a week, my wrist started to feel better. In two weeks, my pain was gone, and I could use my wrist normally again. I haven't had a problem with it since.

I will forever be grateful to Louise for helping me see that I am my own best healer, and for lighting the path in such a loving, inspiring way.

꙰ ꙰ ꙰

The Jolt I Needed
by Margaret, yoga therapist and
workshop leader, Switzerland

Crash! Bang! Wallop! Hearing these sounds while driving one day, all I could think was, *Oh my God! What's happening?* I felt my body being pushed forward and then backward several times, as a car rear-ended me. Over the next few days, I became aware of various aches and pains, particularly in my neck and shoulders. I was also unable to work, which meant that I missed out on the promotion that was about to be offered to me. I told myself, *My life is ruined.* And as I kept saying that to myself, the ruin manifested in my body and in my life. My body was screaming at me, and I felt very alone and very sorry for myself.

Gradually, my healing and transformation began. I started to change my thinking *and* my life. A big influence was reading Louise Hay's *You Can Heal Your Life*, which helped me realize that how I felt and what I thought were up to me. I attended relaxation classes, and although I initially found it really difficult to relax, I kept going because I knew it was important. Then something clicked and I found the fun in it.

I became interested in complementary medicine, having discovered for myself the benefits of a holistic approach. I studied Amatsu therapy, just to find out more about what had helped me personally, never thinking that this could lead to a career change. I also read numerous self-help books and attended many workshops, including the first *I Can Do It!* Conference in Las Vegas. I meditated and did lots of affirmations, saying them out loud, singing them, and writing them down, all while (sometimes rather desperately) trying to listen to my inner wisdom. I made thank-you lists until showing appreciation became second nature. And even though I was fiercely independent, I asked for help to start my own business. Mirror work proved to be very effective in kick-starting my new ventures.

Over the years, my life turned around in many different ways. I became a personal-development workshop leader, an Amatsu and craniosacral therapist, and a yoga teacher. I made a commitment to myself to honor and value my life and to follow my heart. I kept affirming: *My life gets better all the time,* and it became my reality. I also thought, *I am fitter, stronger, and more flexible than ever before in my life* . . . and so I am.

I now live in Switzerland in the house of my dreams with my loving and supportive life partner, surrounded by wonderful friends and neighbors. I work internationally and help people embrace their own vitality to create what they want in life. I feel truly blessed in so many ways. My car accident gave me the jolt I needed—I recognize that it was the gift that has helped me find joy, success, and fulfillment.

☙ ☙ ☙

The Power Is Within Me!
by Iraida, retired, Venezuela

At the end of January 2004 my daughter, Zoimar, brought me to a health class. When I walked in, one of the instructors asked me, "Why are you here?" I told her that I'd like to get rid of my headaches, and she said, "We can do that." There were a lot of books recommended by the instructors, and one of them was *You Can Heal Your Life,* by Louise Hay.

A friend lent me her copy, and once I started to read it, I didn't want to stop. I finished the book in five days, even though I'm not a voracious reader. I started saying affirmations all the time and loved the feeling they brought me. For my birthday that year, my daughter gave me my own copy of *You Can Heal Your Life,* along with *Heal Your Body.* I was so happy.

I became even more interested in Louise, so I bought *The Power Is Within You, Life! Reflections on Your Journey,* and *Empowering Women.* I began to notice changes in my life. For example, I used to depend on pills for my headaches, and now I don't even buy them. Instead, I like to affirm: *I approve of myself* and *The power is within me.*

I thank God for giving me the opportunity to learn all these wonderful things. And I thank Louise for her knowledge. I admire her so much, and hope she continues to share her positive thoughts with everybody. God bless her.

✿ ✿ ✿

The Graceful Flow of Everything
by Saari, consultant, Trinidad and Tobago

In June 2000 I was at a friend's house and saw a brightly colored book on her table. The book was *You Can Heal Your Life,* by Louise L. Hay. I hadn't previously heard of her, but I liked the look of the book and asked to borrow it.

I read the book in random order and was especially fascinated by "the list," which shared the link between a health issue and its probable cause and then suggested a "new thought pattern." The list would prove to be a lifeline for me later that year.

In December, I went in for a "simple and routine" surgery to remove a cyst from my left ovary. Eight hours later, I awoke from the anesthetic in agony. It would take my stomach being swollen for a week before I realized that something was terribly wrong. I began vomiting so violently that I eroded the lining of my esophagus and brought up blood, and there was an excruciating pain in my left side. The initial trip to the emergency room showed that I had *pyelonephritis* (kidney infection).

After weeks of confusion and distress, the final diagnosis was that the laser used to remove the cyst had "misfired" all over my internal organs. The result was a punctured bladder, a damaged kidney, misdirected urine through my vagina and bowels, and an almost completely severed ureter—which meant that urine was also leaking inside my body and had paved the way for sepsis.

The following weeks were a mass of urine bags, leg cramps, spasms, pethidine, morphine, codeine, confused bowels, intravenous pyelograms, CAT scans, stents, and investigative and corrective surgeries. The possibility of a hysterectomy or life with a colostomy bag left me feeling low, then lower, and then at rock bottom. I had bizarre dreams concerning my deceased mother, my guides, and even Archangel Raphael. Tears and prayers were my only comforts as I lived in a nanosecond-by-nanosecond world.

Fortunately, in the middle of everything, it appeared as if energy and time froze around me, and I could see the universe in complete action, or "the graceful flow" of everything. I realized that everyone who would play a healing role for me was either already in my life or had made their remarkable entrance, including my family and friends, who provided strength and support; the patient nurses and the gentle and kind nursing aides; and the doctors who actually made a difference and understood that they were the tools for something, or someone, greater than themselves to create a miracle.

It was after the darkest period that I remembered "the list" and returned to Louise's book. I saw the connection between my health crisis and my thoughts, and understood that I could make the choice to heal myself . . . and I did. I chose to rejuvenate my body and return it to its normal functioning. I chose to smile and laugh. I chose to live a bag- and stent-free existence. I chose to take the lesson and grow. And I chose to forgive, completely. Now, all these years later, I am truly healthy and happy!

ᵜ ᵜ ᵜ

I Choose to Live Joyously and Move Forward
by Bethany, author, Florida

It was the summer of 2006, and I'd hit an all-time low. My heart was aching because I was living in complete isolation and stuck in a physically and emotionally abusive relationship. My body and soul were falling apart—my fibromyalgia had become so bad that I could barely walk. Mostly bedridden, I spent my days trying to find out where I'd gone wrong.

When my abuser was home, I thought about how I wished I could make him stop, but I didn't know how. I feared it was too late, and this terrified me. One night I realized that I'd hit my lowest point, and I knew I must make the choice to live or die. I decided to live.

The next day, by an act of God, I was blessed to have a copy of Louise Hay's *You Can Heal Your Life* in my hands. I started reading, and a spark lit up in my heart. As I read about affirmations, I became excited to start healing my life. I started saying the affirmations immediately. I was addicted! All day, I'd repeat affirmations over and over, including: *I love myself, My body is healing, I forgive myself and others,* and *I trust in life.*

Slowly I was able to stop the abuse and leave this man altogether, and I knew it was time to move on and create something beautiful in my life. I had big dreams, and I'd been offered a great job in California—the only thing holding me back was my knees.

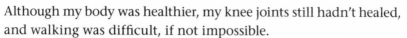

Although my body was healthier, my knee joints still hadn't healed, and walking was difficult, if not impossible.

I was drawn to pick up Louise's book again, and immediately flipped to the page about knees. I read that knee problems represent inflexibility. I realized I was resistant to change because I feared moving forward. *No wonder,* I thought, *since every step I've taken seems to have led me somewhere I didn't want to go.* That day I repeatedly affirmed: *I am flexible and flowing.* The next day, I woke up, put my walker on the sidewalk, and took a light jog. Call it God or coincidence; I call it a true *miracle.* My knees were healed!

I moved to California the next week. For the first time in my life, my soul was free, and before long, all of my dreams started coming true. I am now a writer myself. The flame inside me that I thought had died forever now shines so brightly. (And I still use affirmations every day!)

Louise, you will always be my greatest role model, and for the impact your work has had on my life, I am truly grateful.

⚓ ⚓ ⚓

I Am My Own Miracle!
by Grainne, teacher, New Zealand

I was traveling the world when I met a man whom I really clicked with. We decided to stay together as long as it was fun—our plan was no plan! We had great adventures and got married. After settling in New Zealand, we had a darling little girl (who's now seven). All was well, but I did miss my friends and family, who were thousands of miles away. I visited home when I could, though.

During one of these trips, my mother asked me to come back home to live with her and take care of her in her old age. After discussing it with my husband, we agreed to do so. However, my brother was of a completely different opinion, telling me in no uncertain terms that I was not welcome. As he hurled abuse, I cried like a baby, asking how he could talk to me that way since I was his sister. I really could not understand his anger and felt devastated.

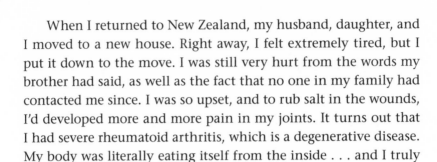

When I returned to New Zealand, my husband, daughter, and I moved to a new house. Right away, I felt extremely tired, but I put it down to the move. I was still very hurt from the words my brother had said, as well as the fact that no one in my family had contacted me since. I was so upset, and to rub salt in the wounds, I'd developed more and more pain in my joints. It turns out that I had severe rheumatoid arthritis, which is a degenerative disease. My body was literally eating itself from the inside . . . and I truly believe that those nasty words were eating me away.

I became so immobilized that I needed help just to take my clothes off, and I was eventually prescribed "superdrugs" to manage the pain. I'd never even taken an aspirin before, and here I was, drug dependent. My body had let me down. I was disappointed in myself, and I felt helpless and stressed to the max.

One day I read *You Can Heal Your Life,* and it really struck a chord. I realized that there was a connection between what went on in my head and what happened in my world. I started my healing process by forgiving my brother. I let go of the hurt and the anger and redirected my attention to *me.* Instead of looking at all the things I could no longer do, I listed everything I *could* do. I started a gratitude journal. I changed my vocabulary and became conscious of the words I used. I told my body that it was natural for it to be well.

Little by little, I got in touch with my inner being. I redirected my attention to the trillions of cells in my body, which were constantly changing, repairing, and improving. My body knew what to do. Before long, I was pain free—and I eventually became drug free, too. I no longer saw my condition as a lifelong disease, and my outlook became happier.

I am now in remission and am full of life. I believe in my ability to allow great things to happen, and I am my own little miracle!

꿈 꿈 꿈

The Art of Living
by Becky, teacher, Israel

I am as I am—how wonderful! My heart sang this message at the beautiful Carmel Forest Spa Resort of northern Israel, where I was leading the "Love Yourself, Heal Your Life" teacher-training workshop.

I was born in Chile to loving Dutch parents; my mother's family had perished in the Holocaust. As a child, I loved to hear the story of how Father fell in love with Mother upon seeing her picture. My soul chose this loving environment of early life, and I was full of joy and self-esteem. I was an actor, dancer, musician, and painter. I remember my excitement when I first fell in love, dancing on the rooftop, feeling beautiful.

At age 11, I contracted what the doctors thought was either polio or meningitis. I remember my father carrying me downstairs to an easy chair, where I waited for friends who never came. Apparently, they were afraid that I might be contagious. I've erased relearning to walk from my consciousness. (Or have I? So many times I feel like I'm going to fall, but then I don't.) I do remember being terrified of every new starting point, be it in school, work, or relationships.

When I was 16, my parents moved us to Israel. Compared with our vibrant life in Chile, I found the country's mentality, teeth-breaking Hebrew language, and dull religious school to be almost impossible to adapt to. Perceiving a world of fear, difficulty, and judgment, I learned to stifle my creativity. Where did that joyful little girl go?

I learned to give the world what I thought it wanted and created a deep ache where my insecurities grew. By the time I was 30, I was a neurotic and unhappy wife and mother, angry at the universe. After the birth of my youngest daughter, my body experienced an earthquake. My right leg started to shorten, I suffered terrible back pain, and my stomach revolted against all of the medication I was taking. I was young and crippled again—after all of those years, my cells still remembered the pain of my childhood illness.

But when the student is ready, the teacher appears. Craving change, I began to trust God and myself, and I went on to explore various healing modalities. I traveled all the way from Tel Aviv to San Diego for Louise Hay's life-training course, "You Can Heal Your Life."

I returned a different person. I could decide what to think, so whenever my mind chattered away, I'd tell myself, *Don't give it another thought.* I renounced guilt trips by choosing my responses to life. Deep inside, I knew I could do it. After two weeks, my life had transformed to the point that I decided to teach the Louise Hay method in Israel myself. I quit our family business and dedicated myself to love.

My body slowly began to change. As I worked on loving myself, the pain diminished. Today I am free of medication. Images of tripping and falling have faded. I walk erect without limping. Life is wonderful, even with its challenges, because my perspective has changed completely. My intention and prayer today is to spread these wonderful tools of healing around the globe. What power we have to heal our beautiful souls!

↙ ↙ ↙

Forgiving and Healing
by Patricia Ann, custodian, Idaho

It was about ten years ago, and I was in the hospital. I had stones in both of my kidneys, and one was on the brink of failure. I was very sick. Doctors tried three different kinds of surgeries to get the stones to pass, but there were two big ones that wouldn't budge. At this point, a good friend brought me *You Can Heal Your Life,* by Louise L. Hay. At first I resisted reading it, but I was so sick that I had nothing better to do. I picked up the book and slowly made my way through it. In the process, this beautiful woman opened my eyes to things I was holding on to from the past, especially my childhood. I decided that it was time to forgive my mother for abandoning me as a child, and I said affirmations regarding this repeatedly. Then I *did* forgive my mother, telling her so in person.

Not long after, one of my doctors asked if I'd passed the two biggest stones, and I said that I didn't remember doing so. He told me that it was impossible for them to just disappear, and if they had passed, I would have felt them for sure. He couldn't believe his eyes, but I was now just fine.

I knew that my affirmations and forgiveness are what helped me pass those kidney stones. Ever since then, I've been making an effort to change and let go. I thank Louise and the friend who brought me her book. I've gone on to find other authors like Louise who have opened my eyes to my spiritual meaning, and today I feel great!

✘ ✘ ✘

My Pain Has Gone "Back to Nowhere"
by Gail, business owner, Canada

Louise L. Hay has touched my life in many subtle ways. I first discovered her more than a decade ago and was then led to other Hay House authors, all of whom inspired me greatly. A couple of years back, I really needed that inspiration. I was going through a divorce at age 40, after being worn down by a critical husband who verbally abused me until I had no self-esteem left. I'd developed arthritis that was so bad I could hardly walk, and I hurt everywhere. He decided to leave me because I was "sick and lazy." We had three young children and a company we ran together. (Adding insult to injury, he left me for a 22-year-old whom I'd hired to help us out for the summer.) I felt as if I'd hit bottom and my world had been shattered.

I was on five medications for the arthritis, and I slowly did feel some relief. Louise's books and CDs were such a comfort during this time, helping me pull myself together. I decided to find out exactly why all of this had happened to me, and to see the blessing in my situation. It wasn't long before I realized that my marriage had been causing me to tell myself, *I cannot stand this anymore.* As Louise says, be careful with your words! My body ended up obeying me, and the arthritis started in my feet. But after I began applying her teachings, it was as if the healing floodgates opened.

Soon I was feeling so much better that I asked my doctor if I could reduce my medication. He said absolutely not. I then attended my first *I Can Do It!* Conference (I've since been to four more) in Las Vegas in 2005. I brought a good friend and had an amazing time. On the flight home, I remembered Louise's words: "It came from nowhere, so send it back to nowhere." That's where I'd send my arthritis—back to nowhere. I no longer needed it. Within a couple months, I had weaned myself off all of my medication and told my doctor, "Thanks for the help, and good-bye." Now when I get an ache or a pain, I'm not afraid; I simply ask myself what's going on in my life that I need to deal with. I rely on my body to tell me, and it always does.

My life is great now. I'm happily divorced; the man who'd treated me so poorly turned into the best ex-husband I could ask for. We still work together every day, and are raising our children together with no quarrels. I'm now engaged to a new love (it's amazing how life treats me better now that I've learned to treat *myself* better, thanks to Louise). And the best part is that I've brought my own daughter Marissa, now 14, to see Louise twice. She loves Louise and Hay House as much as I do.

Louise, thanks for all your love and help, and for bringing so many wonderful authors together for the world to enjoy.

ꗸ ꗸ ꗸ

Strong, Healthy, and Loved Unconditionally
by Tanya, teacher, United Kingdom

All my life I had bad knees, even though I danced regularly as a child. As a little girl, it had been my dream to dance on the stage, but I was told that my knees would never let me do so. The reason I was given was: "It's genetic."

I continued dancing until I was 18, when my right knee gave out and I couldn't walk. I was taken to the hospital and given

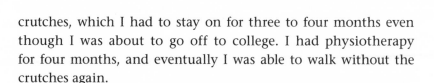

crutches, which I had to stay on for three to four months even though I was about to go off to college. I had physiotherapy for four months, and eventually I was able to walk without the crutches again.

Three years later I was in a crystal shop, and I had some back pain. The owner of the store did some crystal healing on me, but he also advised that I refer to *You Can Heal Your Life,* by Louise Hay. I bought the book and immediately looked up all of the relevant illnesses that I'd had in my life, which amounted to quite a few (I was frequently ill as a child). The words on the pages completely resonated with me: I realized that I had been raised with conditional love, and that everyone around me had been highly critical of themselves and others. I now started the process of learning to love myself, which was incredibly hard. I used affirmations daily (and still do), the most common one being: *I completely love and accept myself.* This powerful statement served to remind me that no matter what anyone else says or does, I *always* love myself.

The healing process was much longer than I had anticipated—but just starting with small steps, such as saying affirmations, really worked. I'd spent so long not feeling loved or accepted, and I was forever seeking other people's opinions and approval. Learning to love myself unconditionally changed my life.

I still get occasional knee pain these days, but now I can tap into the emotion and say my affirmations, and the pain goes away. Quite often after a conflict or situation, my ego tries to take over and say that I'm not worthy, but I just send loving energy to my heart and knees and remind myself that I *am* worthy. Recently I even ran a half marathon, the farthest I'd ever run in my life. I was so proud! A few years ago, I never would have imagined that I could run that far. Lots of people asked me if my knees were hurting, but they weren't. Yes, I had some sore muscles, but no pain. I was incredibly pleased to feel so strong and healthy.

When Louise says that "you can heal your body" and "you can heal your life," she really means it. I have a new life and a happy, healthy body. I feel like a different person! I can't thank Louise enough for teaching me about the power of love.

❦ ❦ ❦

A Wonderful Gift
by Gladys, actor and life coach, New York

On a Saturday morning ten months ago, I woke up in tears. The slightest attempt to turn my head caused pain to rocket up through my neck to my head and reverberate in my throat. Between my sobs and my neck screaming bloody murder, getting out of bed took more than ten minutes but seemed so much longer. Somehow I made it to my chiropractor's office, and he diagnosed me with a pinched nerve.

By Sunday, the pain hadn't subsided at all, and it occurred to me that reading or watching something inspirational might help my healing. I hadn't yet unwrapped my brand-new copy of *You Can Heal Your Life, the movie,* so I did that now and sat down to watch it. Once the movie was over, my computer held several typed notes on what I'd watched, and I was on fire with the desire to affirm my wellness and allow the pain to subside. That night, though, the pain was so severe that I cried and cried. I said a little prayer for healing and relief, having no idea how quickly my prayer would be answered.

The next morning I awoke with the clear understanding that this transient pain was an opportunity for me to learn to be happy despite what was happening in my life. In other words, this was a spiritual experience, and I needed to plumb it for whatever it was worth.

There was no way I could go to work that day, so I decided to spend it constructively and proactively promoting my healing, starting with reviewing *You Can Heal Your Life* and working with Louise's *What I Believe and Deep Relaxation* CD. I affirmed, prayed, meditated, and wrote in my journal . . . even though all of these practices often ended up as naps. (Remember, I couldn't hold my head upright.) I was in a deep state of knowing and believing in my well-being and my own goodness.

That night I went to bed certain that my healing had not only begun, but was in full force. I fell asleep listening to Louise's voice on the *Deep Relaxation* CD, assured that my power lay in the present moment and that all was well. The next morning, I awoke with the knowledge that I was better. Indeed, a profound healing had taken place—there was a completely different quality to the stiffness in my neck! I smiled as I lay in bed, able to turn a couple of inches to the right and a few to the left. I knew that by getting out of my own way and listening to Louise guide me, I was able to activate my own magnificent healing potential.

Yes, ten months ago, I woke up with a stiff and painful neck, but it turned out to be a wonderful gift. Although it may not have seemed like something I'd want to receive, it gave me the tremendous healing potential of Louise's words and allowed me to grow in many more unimaginable ways!

Doing the Work with Louise

I wouldn't call myself a healer. I do not heal others—I simply teach them to love themselves. They are the ones who are doing the true work of healing. However, this doesn't mean people have to do all the work by themselves!

It is not weak to ask for support from friends, family members, or medical professionals. Just remember, the path to healing has to begin from within. If you do not accept health in your mind, you will not accept it in your physical being. The following exercises will help you examine your beliefs about pain and your body. Write your answers on a separate piece of paper or in your journal.

Your Feelings about Your Body

Answer the following questions as best you can:

1. What did you learn about your body as a child?

2. What did your parents teach you about the human body?

3. If you could change anything about your body, what would it be?

Your Beliefs about Pain

Next, answer the following questions as openly and honestly as you can:

1. What are the most negative thoughts you have about your body and the pain you feel?

2. Where did these thoughts come from?

3. Are you willing to release them?

Mirror Work

Look into the mirror and say: *"I am willing to love my body."* Say it several times, with different meanings and emphases each time. Do you agree with this statement? Why or why not?

Look into the mirror again and say: *"I release the need for anything that does not nourish and support me."* Pay attention to how your body feels when you say this.

Letting Go

Now take a deep breath. As you exhale, allow the tension to leave your body. Let your scalp, forehead, and face relax. Your head doesn't need to be tense in order for you to read. Let your tongue, throat, and shoulders relax. You can hold a book with relaxed arms and hands. Do that now. Let your back, abdomen, and pelvis relax. Let your breathing be at peace as you relax your hands and feet.

Can you feel a noticeable change in your body since you started reading the previous paragraph? In this relaxed, comfortable position, say to yourself, *"I am willing to let go. I release. I let go. I release all pain. I release all tension. I release all discomfort. I release all fear. I release all anger. I release all guilt. I release all sadness. I let go of old limitations. I let go, and I am at peace. I am at peace with myself. I am at peace with the process of life. I am safe."*

Go over this exercise two or three times. Repeat it whenever thoughts of pain come up. Soon, the practice will be a part of you. You will be able to reach this state of peace no matter what is going on in your life.

The Power of Affirmations

Affirmations can be powerful tools in counteracting any of your beliefs that support pain. Writing an affirmation can intensify its power. On another sheet of paper or in your journal, write

a positive affirmation about your body 25 times. Create your own, or use one of those listed below.

Affirmations

I create peace in my mind, and my body reflects this.

I am filled with life and energy and the joy of living.

My body is perfectly sound, and I enjoy each new moment.

*I claim my own power and lovingly create my own reality.
    I trust the process of life.*

I lovingly take care of my body, my mind, and my emotions.

I take responsibility for my own life. I am free.

I love my body. I love myself. All is well.

*I process all new experiences easily and incorporate them into
    my life with joy.*

It is safe for me to be who I am.

I see my patterns, and I choose to make changes.

I am willing to go beyond my own limitations.

*I now choose to create a body that is strong and whole.
    I am at ease.*

I easily release what I no longer need. I deserve to feel good.

I heal rapidly, comfortably, and perfectly.

*My body wants to be well. I listen to its messages and treat
    it with kindness.*

I create only joyful experiences in my loving world.

I release the need to criticize my body.

I am willing to create new thoughts about myself and my life.

Every day I am getting stronger and stronger.

I love and cherish myself. I am kind and gentle with me.

Treatment for Pain and Injury

I recognize my body as a good friend. Each cell in my body has Divine Intelligence. I listen to what it tells me and know that its advice is valid. I am always safe, Divinely protected and guided. I choose to be healthy and free. All is well in my world.

Overcoming Addictions

Drugs and alcohol are not the only things a person can be addicted to. Gambling, shopping, food, and even relationships can be the focus of an addiction. Often we look for validation from these other sources because we do not feel love or approval for our own selves. Sometimes we blame another person or a situation for making us the way we are. But nothing in the past can ever be as powerful as what we choose to do in the present moment.

When you truly desire change, you can make it happen for yourself. Of course, you don't have to do it all alone. Help can come from friends, family, mental-health professionals, and support groups.

I hope you feel inspired and moved by the strength of the people in the following stories.

Dancing in the Game of Life

by Claire, jeweler and inspirational teacher, New Zealand

I'd just celebrated my birthday when I woke up with most of my clothes missing and bruises all over me. The withdrawals were more intense than ever, the hallucinations were frightening, and I was so paranoid that I couldn't leave my house.

I had started drinking at age 14. Since I was very shy and with-drawn, it was the perfect medication to escape the world. Ten years had gone by, and I was now in total despair. Two days after my 24th birthday, my boyfriend tried to strangle me—when my roommate arrived home and interrupted it, I got out of the house and never went back. Homeless, jobless, with a long history of sexual abuse and addiction, I was at rock bottom. I was so terrified that suicide seemed like a good option, but I just couldn't do it.

All I had to my name was a bag of clothes and a book called *You Can Heal Your Life*. When I started reading it, a door to a whole new world opened. Something about it just resonated with my soul—it felt like the truth. Although I'd spent a decade under the influence of drugs and alcohol and hated myself without them, I immediately booked myself into rehab to deal with my addictions.

I was so insecure that I couldn't even cross the street without my whole body shaking. I began to do affirmations quite obses-sively, writing them down and saying them as I looked in the mir-ror. Then I started to say them in front of people in rehab. They thought I was a fruitcake, but I had an overpowering knowledge that this was what I had to do.

Within months I noticed a huge change in myself. I also saw a huge change in how others treated me, which I learned I was responsible for. I began to see how my internal dialogue was cre-ating my reality. Consequently, I learned how to look at my past, take responsibility, and change my perceptions, finding the gift in what I thought was misery. Louise Hay's book was the pot of gold at the end of my rainbow.

I am still growing and evolving. I still do affirmations along with meditation, moving from strength to strength. I now listen to my soul, and it's been amazing to see the doors that have opened for me. I've gone from a depressed, dysfunctional, homeless, un-employable human being to an inspired, powerful, free, Divine soul having a human experience and dancing in the game of life. My intention now is to work with addicts using the tools I've learned, and I feel so privileged to be able to help others find their own Divine light within.

✹ ✹ ✹

How I Quit Smoking

by Teresa, artist and writer, Oregon

I was a light smoker for 30 years, on and off. After my divorce at age 50, however, I became a confirmed, pack-a-day smoker for several years. I was definitely hooked. I couldn't quit and wasn't even sure I wanted to—but I *had* to, for health reasons.

I purchased a very expensive prescription drug that was supposed to curb nicotine cravings. The bonus was that I could smoke during the month or so that it would take for the drug to become effective. Two weeks after starting this drug, I was puffing away, wondering how long it was going to take to give the cigarettes up. I still didn't have the slightest desire to quit.

Louise's book *You Can Heal Your Life* was lying next to me at the time, and I remembered that she had a "smoking section" in it, so I went right to it. She'd written:

> You might ask yourself a series of questions like: "Am I willing to give up uncomfortable relationships? Were my cigarettes creating a smoke screen so I wouldn't see how uncomfortable these relationships are? Why am I creating these relationships?"

Those questions hit me like a ton of bricks. I thought of my friendship with a woman who was opinionated, negative, and highly critical; and then I thought about my marriage, where everything had supposedly been my fault. Louise continued:

> Then you notice the reason you're so uncomfortable is that other people always seem to be criticizing you. . . . You then think about criticism, and you realize that as a child you received a lot of criticism. That little kid inside of you only feels "at home" when it is being criticized. Your way of hiding from this had been to create a "smoke screen."

I flashed to my childhood, especially to the parents who'd stamped their "Good Housekeeping Seal of Disapproval" on just about everything my siblings and I said or did. Nothing was ever good enough for them.

I had an epiphany! Stubbing out my half-smoked cigarette, I grabbed the remainder of the pack and ceremoniously crushed every one of them into a pile and announced, "I am willing to release the need to be criticized."

I quit smoking that day and never took another pill from the prescription. Quitting was easy, so I was ready to start being easy on myself. Since then, I have continued my healing journey and have found new relationships that support me in my truth. Before, when I believed I wasn't good enough, I attracted plenty of people to support that belief. Smoking provided the shield that kept me from seeing the truth.

Now, I watch how I talk to myself and about others. I've learned that if I criticize someone else, I'm just criticizing myself. I like me too much to practice that old self-loathing behavior. It just doesn't fit anymore!

꒰ ꒰ ꒰

My Second Chance
by Irena, student, Australia

When *You Can Heal Your Life* was first given to me, it was as if someone had sent me an angel in my time of need. No one prior to this had ever cared enough to give me anything so special, so I accepted the book gratefully. I had a difficult time reading it at first because I couldn't comprehend why I should be given a second chance . . . and I didn't believe that I deserved it. It took a while, but I did read the entire book. When I finished, I felt sick of the life I was living and knew I wanted that second chance. I realized that I had so much to give to the world, and if I could make the transformation within myself, then anyone could.

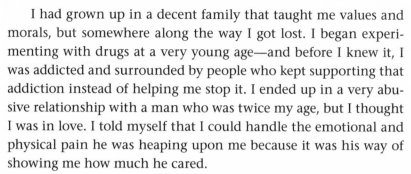

I had grown up in a decent family that taught me values and morals, but somewhere along the way I got lost. I began experimenting with drugs at a very young age—and before I knew it, I was addicted and surrounded by people who kept supporting that addiction instead of helping me stop it. I ended up in a very abusive relationship with a man who was twice my age, but I thought I was in love. I told myself that I could handle the emotional and physical pain he was heaping upon me because it was his way of showing me how much he cared.

One day, this man got himself into a lot of financial trouble and encouraged me to help him out. At the time I would have done anything for him, and I did. Before I knew it, I was prostituting my body for 12 hours a night, five days a week, and handing thousands of dollars at a time over to him. The money was never enough, though, and the abuse got worse.

After months of the same routine as a sex worker, I realized that the man I loved did not love me back. I began talking to other prostitutes and found that there was a support network among them. I couldn't talk to my mother because I was ashamed and had already hurt her so much, so I talked to the girls at work. That's where I found the angel who gave me Louise's book, and in it I found my inspiration. Ultimately, I gathered the strength to leave this man and get off drugs.

I am now going to college, studying psychology, and living back home with my family. I have remained sober, and most of the time I am so happy. Whenever I do get bouts of depression, I just tell myself that "all is well in my world," and I surround myself with the positive energy that Louise has taught me to find. My life has changed so dramatically, and I am thankful for that every day. I'm looking forward to getting my degree in the next couple of years, and I know that nothing can stop me from achieving all of my goals and desires!

✍ ✍ ✍

I Love and Approve of Myself
by Bryan, spiritual life coach, California

I love and approve of myself. When I first heard those words, I thought, *What the hell are you talking about?* They made no sense; in fact, they seemed impossible to fathom for this twentysomething, HIV-positive, dry drunk who hated himself and blamed the entire world for his problems. See, I wore my "V for victim" like a medal of honor. My anger and frustration with my life permeated almost everything I attempted, and absolutely blocked any sustainable good from my life. To say that I was irritable, restless, and discontent would be putting it mildly. I was profoundly unhappy, filled with rage and hopelessness. But here is the key: I wanted to change. I just had no idea how.

I first learned about Louise Hay when I was diagnosed with HIV in 1988. I was told that she held a Wednesday night "Hayride" in West Hollywood, which was a support group for men and women whose lives had been affected by HIV/AIDS. I decided to go, and what I saw changed my life.

I can remember that what Louise was offering at the time was *not* being offered by the media, which spouted fear about the disease; or by Western medicine, which pretty much told you HIV was a death sentence. And for many at the time, it was. Even so, Louise was out there on the front lines, offering hope.

What I witnessed and felt at my first Hayride of about 500 men and women is hard to describe. But I can say it felt unusually familiar to my soul. I was profoundly touched by Louise's words that "we're not going to come together to play 'ain't it awful.'" In her gentle, loving, matter-of-fact way, she shared a very simple message: "No one's coming to save you, but you can save yourself." I felt a sense of safety, trust, and love in this powerful group Louise had created.

I can pinpoint the beginning of my shift in consciousness to these Hayrides. Truth is, I thank God for the day I was introduced to Louise. Her books, lectures, and enlightened teachings have truly altered and shaped the last 20-plus years of my life. Today, I am still an avid follower of Louise and her work. The gifts she's

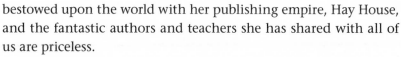

bestowed upon the world with her publishing empire, Hay House, and the fantastic authors and teachers she has shared with all of us are priceless.

I am a happy, strong, healthy, and successful man. I have almost 20 years of sobriety by the grace of God and the 12 steps. I have chosen to live Louise's teachings and apply them to all areas of my life, most powerfully through the practice of daily affirmations. And it all started with a simple mantra I heard years ago: *I love and approve of myself.*

God bless you, Louise Hay.

✕ ✕ ✕

My Future Is Bright
by Helene, administrative assistant, Canada

Louise Hay gave me a lifeline at the beginning of my healing journey. I'd suffered so many losses, including my house, my husband, and my money—not to mention the passing of friends to cancer and the deaths of my parents and a sibling. Past experiences of abuse had left me believing that this was the life I deserved. I was left in total despair, lost in the clutches of alcohol and drug abuse. Yet as a single mother, I knew I couldn't continue living like this. I have two beautiful daughters—my angels!—who count on me, so I had to be a good role model for them.

I picked myself up with the help of Louise's wonderful books, suggested readings, and daily affirmations. I now live by her words, and this has transformed my life! I'm living in a new city, starting fresh in every sense of the word. It didn't happen overnight (this was a six-year journey), but here I am *today!* I'm employed by an incredible company, and I work with the most amazing and positive colleagues. I'm taking care of my body as the temple it is and truly *living* life with eyes wide open to all its beauty. Never does a day go by when I'm not grateful for the lessons Louise has taught me. I encourage everyone to take heart: Life is what you make of it, so don't despair! Even the bad experiences can be changed into positive contributions to your "being."

My future is bright, and I attribute this to you, Louise! My biggest wish is to someday attend one of your sessions in person and get to thank you personally for all you've brought to my life. You are a blessing!

⚰ ⚰ ⚰

Yes, I *Can* Heal My Life!
by Abigail, self-esteem life coach, Kentucky

On December 25, 2003, my mom gave me a copy of *You Can Heal Your Life*. Inside, she'd written: "I hope you enjoy Louise Hay's approach to health. She is one of my favorites!" At the time, I was an active alcoholic who was also addicted to drugs; suffering with my weight and sexuality because I'd been raped; and numb to the reality that my body was about to be cut open only to be remade, as society preferred it to be, with plastic surgery.

Being a victim when convenient had become comfortable. Playing the role of polished public leader while secretly feeling isolated and lonely had become normal in my life. I needed Louise's words, but I could not hear or feel at this point in my life, nor did I like to read. Thankfully "the list" in *You Can Heal Your Life* briefly touched on common diseases. Since it was so simple to navigate and held powerful keys for improving one's immediate mental state, I was sold. Almost.

After reading the book, I made lists about loving my body, believing I was whole, talking to myself in the mirror, blah, blah, blah. I slid back into old patterns, never practicing my affirmations for more than a day. I was Jekyll and Hyde, a depressed leader with beauty and self-doubt. Life remained painfully comfortable.

One day I woke up in jail with my face and knees covered in bruises and crusty blood, thanks to my attempt to beat up police officers while inebriated the night before. I was arrested up against a car, which took my memory back to how I'd been raped several years earlier. I don't recall the physical details, but the emotions are vivid. I knew I was cruel when the officers stripped me of my diamonds and pearls, when they placed me in an all-white "crazy person" room, and when I woke up and realized it was real. The person I was now looking at in this hazy mirror was not the one I'd intended to become.

When I got home, I picked up *You Can Heal Your Life* again. I kept repeating the phrase, "Me? *I* can heal my life?" I was so scared, but for the first time, I believed that, yes, I could. God needed me to be a voice for others, and this meant I would no longer use Band-Aids; I was going to physically, mentally, spiritually, and emotionally heal. I accepted the new thought patterns in the book and trusted in a fraction of Louise's words.

For years, I'd given advice to other people, but stepping into responsibility for my own self was in a new league. By being true to her purpose, Louise helped *me* live on purpose. Louise's affirmations (along with Wayne Dyer's intentions) gave me a new beginning.

Since 2005, I've traveled to learn, but I've stayed put to teach. Today, I am sober, spiritual, successful, and courageous. I am a life coach to high-school and college women; with Louise's affirmations, my experiences, and the power of the Universe, we improve lives.

ᴋ ᴋ ᴋ

The Light at the End of a Long, Dark Tunnel
by Mary Ellen, reflexologist and group facilitator
in personal development, Ireland

In the mid-1980s, I experienced one of those "clearing house" episodes that seem to occur to strip us down and make us more receptive to ego release and spiritual awakening. I lost my job and home, my partner took off with someone more beautiful and accomplished, and I became alienated from my dying mother. Reacting to all of this, I lost my connection with Spirit—and myself.

I developed a drinking problem, became very promiscuous, gave up on a professional career for which I'd trained for four years, lived hand to mouth, and seemed to lose my moral compass. Behavior that would have been unacceptable to me throughout the previous 30 years of my life now became the norm. I pretty much tried to throw my life—and myself—away.

That long, dark tunnel persisted for almost five years. Many times I was suicidal: I had two deliberate car accidents, had alcohol poisoning, and abandoned myself drunk in dangerous places. Twice I was arrested and held overnight. I'd abandoned all my stable connections, and the people who were currently in my life were all more or less lost as well.

One beautiful day I woke up on the futon in a compassionate friend's house. The level of desperation was almost overwhelming at that time; I felt as if I had nothing. I decided to go for a walk to a kind of hidden-away bookshop in a leafy area. It was one of those sacred spots where everything in it gives a little chime of Spirit. I looked at everything in the shop, and I bought *You Can Heal Your Life.* I went on to study it carefully, do the work it called for, and develop a bond with Louise that was the only one I had with anything good at all.

It has been a long, slow process that took an often-tough 20 years. But today, I have a beautiful home in a peaceful place, a loving husband, a career I can feel proud of, and a constant stream of goodness coming into my life. I am in touch with Spirit, and every day I move closer to that Oneness of All that is sacred. My thanks to Louise are impossible to express. I have shared her work with hundreds of people now through my own work, and continue to pass on her wisdom. I probably always will. And I definitely will always love her and have unlimited gratitude.

᠕ ᠕ ᠕

Salvation

by James, writer, Canada

My introduction to Louise Hay happened the summer of 1995 when a co-worker began to "rave" about *You Can Heal Your Life*. Something spoke to me in that moment, and I immediately went out and bought a copy. I was looking for something, but I wasn't sure what. Maybe it was salvation.

A shift began when I picked up my copy of Louise's book that fateful summer afternoon. I knew it had "power," so instead of diving right in, I chose to put it away and get high instead. During that time I was a serious drug abuser. I was scared, lonely, and had absolutely no self-esteem; drugs provided a temporary escape from my reality. In my drug-induced states I could become someone who wasn't scared of anything, and I could shine like a spotlight in the presence of others. Happiness would fill me to my core . . . until the drugs would wear off and I'd begin the slide back downward. I believed that I was unlovable and tried to fill the void in my heart by going to bed with many, many men.

After spending three days awake (I was so drugged up that sleep was impossible), I pulled out *You Can Heal Your Life*. I read it cover to cover. Then I read it again, and once again. At that point I fell into a peaceful sleep for 36 hours. Upon waking, I looked around my room. Everything seemed a little brighter and more colorful than I could ever remember. Next to me on the bed was Louise's book. Picking it up once again, I really started to absorb the material inside. I said the affirmations out loud to myself, and then I ran to the bathroom to say them in the mirror, to my face—a face that, for the first time in my life, didn't repulse me.

Everything changed for me that day, beginning with the choice I made to stop abusing myself with drugs. It wasn't easy, since my friends left with the drugs, but light slowly began entering my soul. I continued to lose myself in Louise's book and practice affirmations every day. Over the months I became healthy and strong and began enjoying the art of living. I finally started liking myself.

All these years later, the fear is gone—excitement has taken its place. I live my life in love, presence, and joy. I now love myself and excel at everything I try. I lead an amazing, wonderful, fulfilling life . . . one that I am grateful for each and every single day.

Louise, you are a gift from the Universe. Your books and teachings come from within your beautiful soul. I am honored and humbled to share space with you on this earth. By living in your truth, as well as by putting your energy out into the world every day, you save lives—including my own. Thank you.

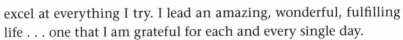

Overcoming Alcohol—and Guilt and Shame
by Kathy Lynn, student, Tennessee

This is the story about a girl who, for as far back as she can remember, dressed herself in guilt and shame. Each morning when she got up, she looked into the mirror at her flaws and inadequacies, and proceeded through the day "should-ing all over" herself.

When I was 25 years old, I discovered alcohol. When I was 35, I discovered Alcoholics Anonymous (AA). I'd been sober for more than two years when I gave birth to my first and only child, a beautiful baby boy. Ironically, just a few months later, during the most rewarding and beautiful time of my life, I found it necessary to drink. I desperately threw myself more fervently into my Christian faith and the rooms of AA. I began a fierce and frantic search—what was going to heal me? All I can say is that I tried and tried and tried. I tried healing, deliverance, and prayer; I tried going to enough AA meetings, getting the right sponsor, doing the steps over and over and over. What was I doing wrong?

Three DUIs and five treatment centers later, I still couldn't stop drinking! Finally I came to the conclusion that the only way to stop drinking was to . . . stop drinking. I was acting insane, doing the same things again and again and expecting different results. I began to reevaluate my beliefs, since they obviously weren't working for me.

Being sober but still suffering with immense guilt and shame, the Universe led me to Louise Hay's book *You Can Heal Your Life* in a Unity Church bookstore. A wonderful thing happened: with Louise's guidance, I began to heal my life! I became hyper-aware of my thoughts. The detoxification process began as I discovered the power of affirmations. As I applied Louise's teachings to my life, I gradually felt as if every cell of my body were being cleansed. Affirmations became my main strategy of defense in attacking the relentless lies I believed about my life and my self.

My fiancé, who introduced me to the Unity Church, never tires of hearing, "Louise Hay this, and Louise Hay that." He knows that a miracle has happened—a healing has taken place. I now understand that everything I've gone through did not happen *to* me, but *for* me. I'm currently working toward my master's degree in counseling, and I have a vision that exceeds me. I know that the Universe has more planned for me than I can possibly comprehend. I'm eagerly looking forward to sharing the transformative power of Louise's philosophy with those who are suffering, and anyone whom the Creator of the Universe places in my path.

Louise, I consider you to be one of my most cherished mentors, and I'm so grateful that I found you. I want to follow in your footsteps to spread the word that the root of all suffering is a lack of self-love; and that self-love, through self-forgiveness and self-acceptance, is the foundation to all healing.

✶ ✶ ✶

Thank God . . . and Louise!
by Joanne, intuitive angel reader
and Reiki master, Canada

I don't exactly remember how I came across *You Can Heal Your Life* by Louise Hay. But I did, and it came at a time in my life when I needed it most. I'd been struggling with alcoholism for many years and even managed to abstain from alcohol for quite a while. But in 2003, that changed for me—I started getting caught up in the addiction again.

I found myself sick and tired of being sick and tired every weekend. I had three children to raise and managed to keep my job, but I was still hurting inside. I was suffering from the grief of losing family members who were close to me and suffering from sexual abuse as a child. I found that I had a lot to deal with, and to do that, I really needed to get real with myself and sober up.

One day I was looking in my bathroom mirror and asked myself, "How do I do this?" Believe it or not, I heard a male voice say, "Stay sober!" I believe that this was the voice of God. It wasn't even the first time I'd heard this—it was actually the third time, and it had always come whenever I was really troubled in my life. Well, I went right back on the wagon. I fell off of it a few times after that, but I kept getting right back on.

Then *You Can Heal Your Life* ended up in my hands, and I took Louise's words to heart. Thanks to her affirmations, I started to change the way I was thinking, and I worked on filling my soul with what it needed. As I began to deal with my personal traumas and truly sober up, I awakened spiritually. Still needing to find out who I was, I was led by Louise's book to her Website and to other Hay House authors who inspired me to discover myself and live my passion.

Today, I no longer work for the sake of bringing money in; as a certified Angel Therapy Practitioner and Reiki master, I work because it is my Divine purpose.

Thank you, Louise, for being such an inspiration to my life, even though we've never even met. I thank God for you.

⚡ ⚡ ⚡

The Power of Re-parenting and Loving My Inner Child
by Paul, licensed massage therapist, Maryland

In my early adult life, I was repeatedly going through everything in a medicated daze of powerlessness and denial as I repeated destructive behaviors and dysfunctional patterns that originated in experiences with my parents and teachers. Over time, studying Louise Hay's book *You Can Heal Your Life* and listening to many of her tapes helped me develop my understanding and knowledge of forgiveness, both for myself and for others.

I understood by my mid-30s—the time when I began reading and studying Louise's work—that everyone including myself had been doing the best they could with what they knew at the time. So slowly, but very surely, I began taking personal responsibility ("The point of power is now") for my health and restoring my sanity by first releasing resentment and blame. And during my ongoing treatment for various addictions, I also made a conscious commitment and practice to love myself and my inner child. Whenever I caught myself in a spiral of negative thinking, which was so often, I'd start repeating many of Louise's affirmations. This was a way of re-parenting myself on many levels, getting the messages and thoughts I wished I'd been given growing up.

Yes, ultimately I did stop drinking and acting out. But what good—and how enduring—would any of that have been if I had never really learned how to love, trust, and care for myself and my inner child?

Thanks to Louise, I ended up acquiring much wisdom and many tools upon which to build my new foundation of love and self-esteem. From this stronger, healthier place, I could start affirming with even greater success that I am a valuable, worthy man capable of attracting abundance, love, creativity, prosperity, and fulfillment into my world. And so it is!

ᛣ ᛣ ᛣ

I Am a Healthy and Happy Sober Woman
by Denise, addictions counselor, New York

I am a 50-year-old female of Italian descent, born to an upper-middle-class family in Marine Park, Brooklyn. In the late '80s, I became very addicted to crack cocaine. I was married with two young daughters, and I ended up losing the right to see them for six months. I went to three different inpatient rehabs during that time and was unable to maintain abstinence. I was in the deepest, darkest time of my life and in tremendous pain.

In February 1989, I discovered the works of Louise Hay and began to affirm: *I am a healthy and happy sober woman, helping many others who suffer with addiction.* In addition, I kept telling myself, *God is with me always.* Before I knew what had happened to me, I was putting together days of sobriety. Days became weeks, and weeks became months.

In 1990, I got a job as a substance-abuse counselor. Today, I run a women's program in an inpatient drug-and-alcohol rehab center, where we use Louise's work to inspire our women to affirm their healing. My two daughters and I have rebuilt our relationship, and I just received a card from my eldest that states: "I know a woman of strength and beauty / I have watched her for years / She is Mother." I am working on a book about my life and couldn't have done any of this without Louise's words of wisdom. She is a true healer.

✶ ✶ ✶

I Now Have Everything I Want!
by Marilyn, businesswoman, Canada

I woke up one morning with a head that felt like cement, the result of too much alcohol and cocaine. I looked over at my boy-friend, who'd recently knocked out my lower teeth, and thought, *I hate my life!*

A friend had given me the Louise Hay book *You Can Heal Your Life* the week before, and that was the beginning. I made a list of all the things that I wanted:

1. A loving, honest relationship
2. A successful business
3. A home in the country
4. To be free from drugs and alcohol

I wrote them in this order, did affirmations in this order, and everything came to me in this order. That was 11 years ago, and today life is fantastic. I've lived with an honest, fun, warm, loving man for the past ten years. We have a very successful import business and travel overseas in the winter months. We live in an old farmhouse by the lake in a small town in Canada. I will be celebrating my sixth year of sobriety in 2010.

You Can Heal Your Life has been my bible. It has given me freedom from my own pain and the courage to change my life. I learned that the point of power is now. I owe my life to Louise and am eternally grateful.

K K K

Louise's Light
by Laurence, event planner, California

Louise Hay changed my life. When I was in my 20s back in 1985, my life was a mess: I'd lost both parents at a young age, I was into drugs, I had no direction or spiritual foundation, and I was an angry young man with no sense of purpose. A work friend invited me to what she described as an amazing "healing circle" of AIDS patients at Plummer Park in West Hollywood, led by a woman named Louise Hay. I hadn't then, nor have I since, contracted HIV, but I was curious about the amazing work I was told about, along with the miracles that were occurring.

I spent hours in these circles, listening to stories of these brave men fighting this dreaded (and, at the time, largely misunderstood and frightening) disease. And I was mesmerized by Louise's simple message of loving ourselves and how our thoughts create our reality. I began to see AIDS from a larger sense—that not only could we eventually eliminate this disease, but that this work might ultimately lead to more compassion and acceptance in the world at large.

I also began to apply those principles to my own life: In short order, I got off drugs, moved to San Francisco, went back to college, started a catering/events firm that lasted 14 years, found love with a wonderful life partner, and miraculously survived a terrifying downfall in my business after 9/11. I closed my business, only to land on my feet back in my hometown of L.A., with a beautiful home near the ocean, a great job, a loving partner of 17 years, and the best dog in the world.

I came from a broken, alcoholic home where I was continually molested; I had terrible issues with self-worth because of my parents, who meant well but were troubled and filled me with negative messages and self-talk; and my life could have easily gone in a completely different direction. But now I find myself healthy and happy at age 50, still loving Louise and saying my daily affirmations, and looking forward to all the goodies that the next half of my life will bring.

I've been able to give to myself and others in ways I could not have imagined as that angry young man those many years ago. Louise changed my life by being a light that helped lead the way. I changed my own life by learning how simple and easy the Universe really is, if you just learn to let go and maintain an attitude of gratitude each and every day.

꒰ ꒱ ꒰

Doing the Work with Louise

No book, much less a single chapter, can fully take the place of therapy and 12-step programs in healing an addiction. However, change begins within. The best programs cannot help you if you are not ready to release your addictions.

It's time to make a new vision of your future and let go of any beliefs and thoughts that do not support it. You can begin this process of changing your outlook by completing the exercises below. Write your answers on a separate piece of paper or in your journal.

Release Your Addictions

Take some deep breaths; close your eyes; and think about the person, place, or thing you're addicted to. Think of the insanity behind the addiction. You're trying to fix what you think is wrong inside of you by grabbing on to something that is outside of you. The point of power is in the present moment, and you can begin to make a shift today.

Be willing to release the need. Say: *"I am willing to release the need for ___food___ in my life. I release it now and trust in the process of life to meet my needs."*

Repeat this every morning in your daily meditations or prayers.

Your Secret Addiction

List ten secrets that you've never shared with anyone regarding your addiction. If you're an overeater, maybe you've eaten out of a garbage can. If you're an alcoholic, you may have kept alcohol in your car so you could drink while driving. If you're a compulsive gambler, perhaps you put your family in jeopardy in order to borrow money to feed your gambling problem. Be totally honest and open.

Releasing the Past

Now let's work on releasing the emotional attachment to your addiction. Allow the memories to just be memories. As we let go of the past, we become free to use all of our mental power to enjoy this moment and create a bright future. We don't have to keep punishing ourselves for the past.

1. List all of the things you're willing to let go of.

2. How willing are you to let go? Notice your reactions and write them down.

3. What will you have to do to let these things go? How willing are you to do so?

The Role of Self-Approval

Since self-hatred plays such an important role in addictive behavior, we will now do one of my favorite exercises. I've shared this exercise with thousands of people, and the results are phenomenal.

Every time you think about your addiction for the next month, say over and over to yourself, *"I approve of myself."*

Do this three or four hundred times a day. No, it's not too many times. When you're worrying, you'll go over your problem at least that many times in a day. Let *I approve of myself* become a waking mantra, something that you say over and over to yourself, almost nonstop.

Saying this statement is guaranteed to bring up everything in your consciousness that is in opposition. When a negative thought comes into your mind, such as *How can I approve of myself? I just ate two pieces of cake!* or *I'll never amount to anything*—or whatever your negative babble may be, *this* is the time to take mental control. Give this thought no importance. Just see it for what it is—another way to keep yourself stuck in the past. Gently say to this thought, *Thank you for sharing. I let you go. I approve of myself.*

Remember, thoughts of resistance can have no power over you unless you choose to believe them.

Cleaning Up Addictions

Addictions suppress emotions so that we don't feel. If we don't want to deal with what's in front of us, or if we don't want to be where we are, we have a pattern that keeps us out of touch with our lives. It can be a food addiction, a chemical addiction, or an emotional addiction. Maybe we're addicted to running up bills or to getting sick.

If you're going to be addicted to anything, why not be addicted to loving yourself? You can also be addicted to doing something that is supportive of you, such as doing affirmations. Feel free to create your own or use those in the list below.

Affirmations

*I release the pattern in me that created this. I am at peace.
    I am worthwhile.*
It is safe for me to take charge of my own life. I choose to be free.
I release my stress with deep breathing.
I lovingly take back my power. I release this old idea and let it go.
I give myself permission to change.
No person, place, or thing has any power over me. I am free.
I create a new life with new rules that totally support me.
The past is over. I choose to love and approve of myself in the now.
*All experiences are perfect for my growth process. I am at peace
    with where I am.*
*My mind is cleansed and free. I leave the past and move into the
    new. All is well.*
I easily and comfortably release that which I no longer need in life.
I am doing the best I can. I am wonderful. I am at peace.
I freely and easily release the old and joyously welcome the new.
I am willing to change and grow. I now create a safe, new future.

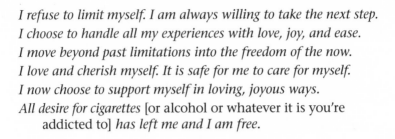

I refuse to limit myself. I am always willing to take the next step.
I choose to handle all my experiences with love, joy, and ease.
I move beyond past limitations into the freedom of the now.
I love and cherish myself. It is safe for me to care for myself.
I now choose to support myself in loving, joyous ways.
All desire for cigarettes [or alcohol or whatever it is you're
    addicted to] *has left me and I am free.*

Treatment for Addictions

*I claim high self-worth and self-esteem for myself. I love and appreciate
myself on every level. I am not my parents, nor any addictive pattern
they may have had. No matter what my past may have been,
now in this moment I choose to eliminate all negative self-talk
and to love and approve of myself. I am my own unique self,
and I rejoice in who I am. I am acceptable, lovable, and Divinely
inspired. This is the truth of my being, and I accept it as so.*
All is well in my world.

Part II

Daily
Life

Chapter Four

Attracting Prosperity

Prosperity is not determined by the size of your bank account; it is determined by your state of mind. What do you feel you "deserve" from the Universe? Do you believe that opportunities pass you by because you're "not good enough"? Belief in lack is the only thing that can limit you. When you change your mind's focus to appreciation for what you have and affirm that you <u>do</u> deserve prosperity, you will be amazed by the generosity that Life has to offer.

The following stories demonstrate the endless abundance of the Universe.

Our Dream Home
by Jacqui, publicity director, California

It was January 2004 and the housing boom was at its height in San Diego. For three months, my husband, Cameron, and I had been looking for just the right house, to no avail. Everything we looked at was too small, too expensive, in a bad location, too much work . . . something always seemed to be not quite right. So, I decided to tape one of Louise's affirmations to my computer screen:

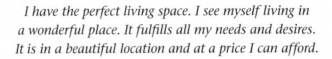

*I have the perfect living space. I see myself living in
a wonderful place. It fulfills all my needs and desires.
It is in a beautiful location and at a price I can afford.*

Just two months later, my husband and I found our perfect home! It had everything we were looking for—and at the right price! We put our offer in, but at the last minute the seller pulled it off the market. We were devastated because we wanted the house so much. I had my real-estate agent contact the seller and let him know that if he decided to sell again, he should be sure to call us.

I was determined to get that house, so I continued to say my affirmations—and I'd even drive by the home at lunch and picture myself living there. I'd also imagine how it would feel to push my children's strollers down the streets in the neighborhood. I could actually *see* my family living there, laughing and talking to neighbors. I fervently repeated Louise's affirmations.

Cameron and I continued our house search and kept asking our agent if the seller of the first house wanted to sell, but the answer was always no. We eventually found another place that came close to our criteria, but we weren't nearly as excited about it as we'd been about the first one. When we went to put an offer on the second house, I had our real-estate agent call the seller of the "perfect home" and ask him one more time if he wanted to sell to us, before we went ahead and purchased this second house. I just couldn't give up. The seller's agent responded with a firm *no!* So I said *more* of Louise's affirmations. I could still see and even *feel* myself living in that house and being part of the neighborhood.

So we put an offer in on the second house. When the sellers countered our offer, it was to our amazement that our real-estate agent told us that the seller of the first house had a business opportunity and needed a lot of cash quick . . . and if we were still willing, he would sell his house to us.

Papers were signed on that miraculous day of April 1, 2004 (no April Fools' joke!), and my husband and two daughters and I couldn't be happier!

❧ ❧ ❧

Attracting the Best with Louise

by Suzanne, human-resources director, Texas

Louise Hay has long been a great inspiration for me and those around me. My first knowledge of Louise's work came in 2000, when I received the book *You Can Heal Your Life* from a friend the day before exploratory surgery. It made perfect sense to me that if a limiting thought has been around a long time, your body will reflect that thought pattern. Therefore, changing your thought pattern to get different results was easy to accept. So I did.

Over the years, I purchased many of Louise's books, CDs, and affirmation cards to support me on my path. I learned to live with an open heart, stop the chatter in my head, and share my self-discovery journey with others. Louise gave me "permission" to invite creativity into my life and the courage to explore, so I now assist others in identifying their passion and living their dreams. I provide guidance by sharing the way I changed my own thoughts.

The affirmations that seem to bring a big smile to everyone are: *I am a magnet of money, and prosperity of every kind is drawn to me.* One day a friend and I were at a bookstore in Scottsdale, Arizona, picking up one of Louise's books, and the cashier smiled and said, "I just love Louise Hay." We replied, "We do, too!" Then all three of us said that we especially like the affirmation *I am a magnet of money.* At that moment, I realized that those who seem to be strangers aren't when it comes to Louise.

I recently bought *You Can Heal Your Life, the movie;* and I really enjoyed hearing more about Louise's life journey and how she's led her life with an open heart. I'm so glad that she followed her heart and decided to share her ideas and thoughts with the world, especially when others didn't think that what she pursued would work.

Louise has given me the courage to explore and experience new opportunities. Whenever I don't feel comfortable in a situation, I am sure to tell myself, *I am safe.* This clears my mind, and I'm able to look objectively at the choices that are before me. In addition, I like the evening meditation she has created: *The day is done, whether it was a good day or a bad day. It is over.* Yes, Louise Hay changed my life and the lives of so many people around me. I can't thank her enough.

✗ ✗ ✗

My Dreams Come True
by Michelle, piano teacher, Massachusetts

I'd been working as a secretary for 11 years when my son was born. I wanted to find a way to stay at home with him and still be able to make money, so I decided to become a day-care provider. My husband was very supportive and encouraged me to make that change. I had this job for two years but felt that I was meant to do more with my life. After my daughter was born, I had a great desire to be a piano teacher, but I couldn't see how that could happen. Although I was a classically trained pianist, I felt that I didn't have the background to teach.

It was 1989, and I discovered Louise Hay. After reading and working with her books and using her wonderful tapes, I began to affirm the life I wanted. I worked on releasing those things from my past that no longer served me. I started to attend workshops and classes that would help me learn how to teach piano. I subscribed to piano-teaching magazines and put an ad in the paper. I soon had seven students, whom I taught in the evenings after my day-care children left for the day. During the next six months, piano teaching became more and more important to me. I continued to read and affirm every day, and felt that I was on the right path.

Little did I know that by affirming what I wanted and truly believing that I could change my life, in ten years I'd not only be a Nationally Certified Teacher of Music and a successful piano teacher, but I'd also be president of the Music Teachers Association in my state. I then became interested in the field of music technology and met some wonderful teachers and mentors. In 2003, I was asked to give my first presentation on music technology at a national conference of music teachers in Utah.

To date, I run a piano studio of more than 50 students; serve on the board of both my state and local Music Teachers Associations; and have presented sessions on music technology at national conferences of music teachers in nine different states, as well as Canada. In addition, I judge festivals held by area piano teachers; I've had articles and reviews published in music-teaching magazines (those same magazines that I subscribed to early on!); and I recently co-authored a book on music technology, which was released this year. I'm a church organist, the director of both the children's and handbell choirs, and the accompanist for many choral groups as well.

Meeting and working with Louise through her books and tapes was truly miraculous for me, as it helped make my dreams come true!

⚜ ⚜ ⚜

Miraculous Healing on Every Level
by Kathryn, spiritual life coach and
personal organizer, Washington

Seven years ago, when I was faced with an operation to remove six fibroid tumors, Louise's book *You Can Heal Your Life* came to me. At the time, I was separated from my husband and deeply entrenched in victim mode. I didn't have a job yet had two mortgages, so I wanted to sell my house in Florida quickly. I needed a miracle, and fast! Thanks to *You Can Heal Your Life*, I was inspired to ask for those miracles . . . and I got them!

Before submitting to an operation (for which I had no health insurance), I asked my doctor if it was true that we could heal ourselves. She simply said, "I *have* seen miracles." I asked her for six weeks to attempt to heal myself of these tumors, because I believed that the pain of my separation may have been what caused them to show up. My doctor granted me the six weeks, but she also set up the ultrasound and other pre-op plans and scheduled the operation anyway. That very day, I began a practice of walking three miles each day, repeating Louise's positive affirmation for fibroid tumors as I walked. I practiced with great hope for six weeks.

When I showed up for my next doctor's appointment, I was firmly convinced that something miraculous had happened. And it had. There wasn't even a trace that those six tumors had ever been there. Several doctors were scratching their heads, mumbling about how this just wasn't possible. I knew that a miracle had occurred, and it didn't stop there. I healed myself from my victimhood and my lack of abundance. I also sold my house in two weeks for cash, and I created my own very successful business. I am a prosperous, healthy, and happy woman. One day I hope to write a book detailing my adventures of seven years ago, as well as all of the miracles that have happened since.

✗ ✗ ✗

The Miracle Mortgage
by Nicole, journey practitioner, Texas

I can't begin to express my gratitude to Louise Hay and Hay House books for opening my awareness to the workings of the Universe. It is to these teachings that I attribute my recent miracle.

My husband lost his job on October 31, 2008, and I became very fearful that we'd lose our home with the recent downturn of the U.S. economy. We agreed that we'd put our home on the market on January 1, 2009, not knowing how long it would take to sell. I knew better than to focus on my fears and lack, but I also didn't want to be unrealistic about the situation. I meditated and prayed on the issue and had the inner knowing that everything would work out for our highest good. I relaxed into trust of the Universe, but we still maintained our plans to list our house.

Three days before our deadline, my husband spoke to the bank. He discovered that unbeknownst to us, they'd made an error and we'd been paying double mortgage payments—our home was paid up until April 2010! Without the mortgage payment and with both of our cars paid in full, we are in great financial shape considering

that we're currently unemployed. This mortgage miracle was all we needed to completely turn our situation around! I knew the Universe was on my side, but the Divine perfection and timeliness of this miracle leaves me in awe!

꙰ ꙰ ꙰

My Heart Now Sings!
by Shelley May, workshop leader, Australia

When I discovered the work of Louise Hay, I'd become stale in my career of some 14 years, and I was disillusioned and burned out. I was also continually getting ill, contracting pneumonia for three consecutive years and shingles in my eye, to name just a few of my ailments. I yearned for something better. I wanted to rediscover my passion and make a difference, not only in my own life, but in others' lives as well.

Learning from Louise, I took action instead of sitting around waiting to be rescued. I booked two weeks' vacation, removed all personal effects from my desk, archived all my filing, and even removed my name tag from my desk. People commented that it looked like I wasn't coming back, and I'd just smile and quietly go about what I was doing. Not once did I share my secret with those around me.

I recharged during my time off, constantly affirming that I was ready to leave my current job and take on a role that would "make my heart sing." I started taking care of *me*—since I'd been in constant pain for many months now, needing pain medication just to get out of bed, I booked an overdue medical checkup.

Eight weeks after I returned to the office, I was told that the company was going through a site closure. In just a couple months, I'd be laid off. I did my best to contain my excitement, but inside I was doing a one-woman "wave"—not only was I leaving, but I was leaving with money!

My checkup had led to the discovery of a sizable ovarian tumor, which I called Monty. Given the fact I'd created it, I thought it only right that I should name it. I finished work, went straight to surgery, and received the good news that the tumor was benign. My new life had truly started!

I am now a full-time student, writer, and artist. I recently trained to be a "Heal Your Life, Achieve Your Dreams" workshop teacher, which means that I truly get to do what makes my heart sing!

Life is good—I am prosperous and happy, and I am eternally grateful for Louise's books. They gave me the key to get out of the prison of my own creation. It is so powerful to realize that you can do, be, and change anything. You just have to be brave enough to think it . . . and then believe it!

K̄ K̄ K̄

Manifesting My Perfect Home
by Jenny, graphic designer, California

Eight years ago I lived in a house that was nice, but it wasn't the right one for my family. I wanted a home that had individuality and open space around it, and my friend told me about a property that sounded perfect. It was an old ranch-style house with plenty of land around it, on a beautiful private road lined with trees, in a quiet neighborhood. My friend told me that the owners were also moving soon.

I walked by the house and fell in love with it. I'd long been a fan of Louise Hay, and I decided to apply some of her manifestation tools to make my dream a reality. I took a picture of the house and displayed it on my refrigerator, and every day I imagined myself living there. I took my daughter for a walk in her stroller by it almost every week. I kept visualizing and affirming that this was my family's home.

Finally, my husband and I were able to visit the house and meet the owners. We made an agreement with no Realtors involved and were able to get the house for a good price.

Within exactly one year of my taking that picture, my family and I were living in our new home. However, the place was not without its flaws. It was 35 years old and had never been updated at all, so my husband and I planned to eventually do some remodeling. We told ourselves that we'd do it when we'd lived there for five years. Five years passed, and then six, and it still didn't seem to be the right time for this undertaking. Yet many of the old things in the house were becoming nonfunctional, and it was distressing.

During the sixth year, I knew I needed to take action. I created a vision map that included all of the things I wanted my home to be: beautiful, peaceful, warm, and inviting, with space for people to gather. I also began to visualize how I wanted the house to appear, both inside and out, affirming that this was indeed the way it looked.

By the beginning of my family's seventh year in the house, we began our remodel. We have now created the home of our dreams, thanks to positive thoughts and affirmations!

Doing the Work with Louise

To receive the limitless supply and abundance of the Universe, you must first have a mind-set that accepts abundance. If you do not, then no matter how much you say you want something, you won't be able to allow it into your life. Yet no matter how long you've accepted the belief *I am a failure,* it is only a thought, and you can choose a new one now.

Take a few minutes to focus on the success and prosperity you want to attract into your life by doing the exercises below. Write down the answers on a separate sheet of paper or in your journal.

Your Use of Money

Write down three ways in which you're critical of your use of money. Maybe you're constantly in debt, you can't save money, or you can't enjoy your money.

Think of one example in each of these instances where you *haven't* acted out the undesirable behavior. For example:

- *I criticize myself for: spending too much money and always being in debt. I can't balance my budget.*

- *I praise myself for: paying my bills this month. I make my payments on time and with joy.*

Mirror Work

Stand up with your arms outstretched, and say, *"I am open and receptive to all good."* How does that feel?

Now, look into a mirror and say it again with feeling.

What kinds of feelings come up for you? Does it feel liberating to _____? (You fill in the blank.)

Do this exercise every morning. It's a wonderfully symbolic gesture that may increase your prosperity consciousness and bring more good into your life.

Your Feelings about Money

Let's examine your feelings of self-worth concerning money. Answer the following questions as best you can:

1. Go back to the mirror. Look into your eyes and say, "My biggest fear about money is _____." Then write down your answer and explain why you feel that way.

2. What did you learn about money as a child?

3. In what era did your parents grow up? What were their thoughts about money?

4. How were finances handled in your family?

5. How do you handle money now?

6. What would you like to change about your money consciousness?

An Ocean of Abundance

Your prosperity consciousness is not dependent on money; your flow of money is dependent upon your prosperity consciousness. As you are able to conceive of more, more will come into your life.

Visualize standing at the seashore, looking out at the vast ocean and knowing that it reflects the abundance that is available to you. Look down at your hands and see what sort of container you're holding. Is it a teaspoon, a thimble with a hole in it, a paper cup, a glass, a tumbler, a pitcher, a bucket, a washtub—or perhaps you have a pipeline connected to this ocean of abundance? Look around you and notice that no matter how many people there are and no matter what kind of container they have, there is plenty for everyone. You cannot rob another, and they cannot rob you. And in no way can you drain the ocean dry. Your container is your consciousness, and it can always be exchanged for a larger container.

Do this exercise often to experience feelings of expansion and unlimited supply.

Your Money Consciousness

Now let's examine the issue of self-worth with respect to your financial situation. Answer the following questions. After each one, say one or more of the affirmations that follow to counteract the negative belief.

1. Do you feel worthy of having and enjoying money?
2. What is your greatest fear regarding money?
3. What are you "getting" from this belief?
4. What do you fear will happen to you if you let go of this belief?

Affirmations

I relax into the flow of Life and let Life provide all that I need easily and comfortably.

I am an unlimited being, accepting from an unlimited source in an unlimited way.

I am a magnet for Divine prosperity.

My life is a success.

I always have as much as I need.

I now deserve all good. I allow good experiences to fill my life.

I am blessed beyond my fondest dreams.

I am open and receptive to all the good and abundance in the Universe.

There is a perfect home for me, and I accept it now.

My income is constantly increasing.

I deserve the best, and I accept the best now.

I give myself permission to prosper.

I know that I am worthwhile, and it is safe for me to succeed.

I live and dwell in the totality of possibilities. Where I am there is all good.

Infinite prosperity is mine to share; I am blessed.

I trust that all my needs will be taken care of.

Life is wonderful, all is perfect in my world, and I always move into greater good.

Riches of every sort are drawn to me.

There is plenty for everyone, including me.

I now receive my good from expected and unexpected sources.

Treatment for Prosperity

I am totally open and receptive to the abundant flow of prosperity that the Universe offers. All my needs and desires are met before I even ask. I am Divinely guided and protected, and I make choices that are beneficial for me. I rejoice in others' successes, knowing there is plenty for us all. I am constantly increasing my conscious awareness of abundance, and this is reflected in a constantly increasing income. My good comes from everywhere and everyone. All is well in my world.

Chapter Five

Handling Career Challenges

Each of us is looking for fulfillment, and finding the right career is an important part of doing so. Yet it is so common to hear people complaining about work. They hate their job, can't find a job, don't get along with their boss, aren't making enough money . . . the list goes on and on. Do you often find yourself saying these or similar statements? Remember that whatever position you are in, you drew it to yourself with your thoughts. Let go of your limited thinking, and allow yourself to move forward in the direction that brings you joy.

The people in the following stories share how they created their ideal work situation.

Undreamed-of Possibilities
by Melanie, director of giving, California

I was blessed to meet Louise Hay in the early 1990s. I was thrilled to do so, as I had read her books for years and had shared them with several friends and family members. It was "friends at first sight"! Within a few months, Louise occasionally asked my advice on what nonprofit organizations she could give financial assistance to, and I was happy to share ideas with her. After going to the East Coast for a few years, I was again blessed to be reunited with her upon my return to California. My work at that time was involved with several local organizations; once again, Louise would ask me how Hay House might contribute to the community.

In 2005, after being at a great job helping foster children and working on special events in the community, I found myself increasingly interested in giving to more people in a real and tangible way. So when I created my yearly visualization board, I included a picture of Louise and me standing together, smiling, with our arms stretched out wide. Under the picture I wrote these words: *Undreamed-of Possibilities.* I'd often take out the board and affirm: *I have a wonderful job in every way with wonderful people and wonderful pay, giving wonderful service every day,* which came from Florence Scovel Shinn, one of Louise's teachers.

My affirmation became a reality in 2008, when I was offered the position of Director of Giving for Hay House. I can truly say it was an "undreamed-of possibility," and I have a wonderful job in every way!

I'm so grateful that Louise gave me the opportunity to share her vision to provide people with healing avenues and empowering books to improve the quality of their lives. It is also an honor to travel with her while she continues to teach and share her love, kindness, beauty, and great sense of humor with all who cross her path.

ᛣ ᛣ ᛣ

Nothing Short of Amazing
by Andrea, holistic-health counselor,
natural-foods chef, and author, New York

At age 28, I had a great job and felt on top of the world. Then I was diagnosed with hyperthyroidism, which doctors advised treating with radioactive iodine and Synthroid. I opposed radiation, especially after watching my mother die from breast cancer treated with radiation. I radically altered my diet and lifestyle and was able to heal my thyroid naturally.

Soon after my healing, I began to feel empty and unfulfilled at the end of my workday. A small voice inside me told me to teach what I'd learned so that I could help other people. My desire to teach was strong, but I was afraid of leaving the safety of my job. My fears paralyzed me: *How could I start a business? How would I promote and market myself? How would I pay rent? I'm already living paycheck to paycheck as it is.*

One day I was sitting in a coffeehouse with these negative thoughts running through my head. A man asked if he could join me at my table, and since there weren't any other seats available, I said yes. Noticing my frustration, he asked what was going on in my life. I told him I wanted to quit my job and start a business, but I was scared. He mentioned a woman named Louise Hay and wrote down this phrase for me: *I am safe in the universe, and all life loves and supports me.* He suggested that whenever a negative thought entered my mind, I replace it with that positive one.

For the next three months, the negative thoughts were persistent and bombarded me from both inside and outside my head. Friends and family members had good intentions, but their negative fears mimicked and compounded my own. I kept fighting to improve my thoughts, just as I'd fought to improve my health. I read Louise's books and repeated the affirmation that man had given me over and over again.

I was walking home from work silently repeating my mantra when I got hit hard—not by a taxicab, but by the realization that I really *was* safe in the universe, and all life *did* love and support me. I was so moved that I stopped walking and yelled my affirmation out loud. People within earshot quickened their pace, since I must have looked and sounded as if I'd lost my mind. The truth is, I'd just found it.

The next day, I gave my two weeks' notice. Since then, my life has been nothing short of amazing: I've written two successful books and am on to book number three. I was a featured contestant on Bravo's *Top Chef;* I'm the food expert for a local television station, and I also host a program where I instruct people how to cook for treating or preventing illness; and I teach 2,000 students annually at several different venues. And, best of all, I am safe in the universe, and all life loves and supports me.

Thank you, Louise Hay. I love you.

ϰ ϰ ϰ

A Workplace Miracle
by Telma, personal support worker, Brazil

I was working in the marketing department of an international company when I received an invitation to transfer to another department. Unfortunately, my new manager was such an ogre that no one in the entire company liked him at all. Although I soon learned that everybody was right concerning his personality, I worked with him for three years. It was such a challenge that everyone I knew told me to give up this job. My manager and I had an argument one day, and at that point, I was so tired of the situation that I told him I wouldn't work with him anymore. He convinced me to hang in there until he got back from vacation.

When this man returned to the office, I realized that something was wrong with him—he couldn't walk properly and seemed very sick. After asking what was going on, I learned that he had disk herniation. He was in so much pain that he couldn't walk, and he had to go to the hospital for several days.

When he came back to work, I asked him about the medical diagnosis. He looked at me with so much fear in his eyes that I could feel some compassion. Clearly enduring a great deal of pain, he said that he was a dead man. A surgery was not possible to help him get rid of the discomfort. I looked deeply into his eyes and said that I could help him. He almost begged me to do so.

I told him about *You Can Heal Your Life.* I didn't have the book on me but told him that I could get him a copy in a couple of hours. I went to a nearby bookstore and saw just one copy on the shelf, as if it were waiting for me. Back at the office, I placed the book on the man's desk and told him, very seriously, that he had to read it *and* do all of the appropriate affirmations.

The next day he came to me and said that he'd devoured the book and felt no more pain; in fact, he'd put away all of the medications he was taking. The next week he was a different person—happier, and in no pain at all. He told me that he knew nothing was wrong with him anymore, and he was going to his doctor to confirm it. A few hours later, he returned to the office very happy, saying that tests couldn't find anything wrong in his spine. The doctor couldn't explain how he could have gotten rid of the problem, since the disk herniation he had was very difficult to treat and couldn't possibly have vanished just like that.

Everybody in the company asked me what I had done with my manager. He was so different, more human and kind. This happened 15 years ago; today when I ask how he's feeling, he says that he's never had any kind of problem in his spine again. He attributes his healing miracle to Louise and has purchased many copies of *You Can Heal Your Life* to give to his family and friends.

ᛕ ᛕ ᛕ

Creating a Wonderful New Job
by Melody, employment-services supervisor, Michigan

After a "surprise" divorce, I decided to enroll in college to make a better life for my children and me. It was difficult being a single parent, juggling two jobs, attending classes, and doing homework, but it was definitely worth it. It took six years to earn my bachelor's degree in human-resources administration and another three years of countless interviews and many rejections before finally finding "the" job. And then it took only a few months to realize I was miserable in the job that had taken me so long to find. I was sure that my unhappiness stemmed from the antagonistic environment of this particular manufacturing plant and not the actual position or work. I had never been in such a hostile environment and knew I had to find a less stressful place of employment.

As fate would have it, I didn't have to quit—the company downsized on September 28, 2001. I was living paycheck to paycheck and had no savings or insurance. Even though I did cry, I also felt a sense of relief. My strong faith in a door opening when another closed gave me strength and encouragement.

I'd already overcome many obstacles in my life, such as my father's abandonment, poverty, teenage pregnancy, cancer, my husband's betrayal, and being a single parent. Due to past experiences, I knew without a doubt that good would come from this new "challenge."

I'd previously purchased Louise Hay's *Power Thought Cards* and went home and grabbed one of the cards out of the box. I said out loud, "There's a message on one of these for me." And sure enough, on one side of the card was written: *I now create a wonderful new job.* And the other side stated: *I am totally open and receptive to a wonderful new position, using my creative talents and abilities, working for and with people I love, in a wonderful location and earning good money.* I put the card in my purse and pulled it out many times each day to read and affirm. I truly believed in this message and knew deep within my heart that it would come about.

Six weeks later, I got a human-services position with a government agency, where I would teach job-search skills to the unemployed. The job was a newly created position, working with like-minded people, just five miles from home, and located on the banks of a beautiful river with a boardwalk right outside the door. And the starting wage was more per hour than the previous position. I even became a supervisor within nine months and received a raise.

That was almost ten years ago. I get great satisfaction and a sense of purpose witnessing the results of my instruction and encouragement. It is gratifying to see people come into the office with the weight of the world on their shoulders, yet leave with a spark of hope in their eyes. To know that I've helped those going through very difficult times is rewarding. I not only know, but I *feel*, that I have truly found my niche. Thanks, Louise!

ĸ ĸ ĸ

Finding My Power in the Mirror

by Chronopoulou, nursery-school teacher, Greece

I am 23 years old and have been working as an assistant in a private school close to my house for about two years. From the beginning, my boss told me that if I was exactly what they expected, I'd probably get a promotion in the future. I wasn't expecting too much from this promise, however, and continued working with no big expectations.

I'd had Louise Hay's book *Empowering Women* for quite a while, but it had never been opened. Now I started to read it intently, and I even said affirmations for changes in my life in front of the mirror. Guess what happened? After just a month, I got the promotion! I couldn't believe that it could happen so soon, and I was very happy and enthusiastic about it!

Today, whenever I am afraid of what life or the Universe will bring to me, I immediately go back to the "practice" in the mirror. Isn't it crazy that we have the real opportunity to be happy and have whatever we deserve, but we sometimes forget that it can really be true for us?

I am truly grateful to Louise and for her courage to teach these wise things to people. I look forward to reading her new book and hope that it will soon be translated into Greek.

✎ ✎ ✎

Becoming the Woman I Once Was

by Ann, equine massage therapist
and riding coach, Canada

Years ago when I was a teenage girl growing up in Jamaica, my father and I used to attend Science of Mind meetings, where we studied the works of Ernest Holmes. In the mid-1980s, my father came across Louise Hay's books, and he really liked them, reading from them to our family all the time. Louise changed his life, and his business thrived. As for me, I grew up knowing that my mind was creative and that I was in charge of my own universe. As the years passed, I married and had kids, but as life got ahold of me, I forgot what I'd learned from my father and Louise. I went through a major bout of depression and lost who I was.

When I was in my 40s, I found myself starting to become interested in the authors my dad used to read all those years ago and found Louise's books again, especially *You Can Heal Your Life*. Reading this book for myself taught me the importance of forgiveness, and it's not until I truly forgave certain people in my life that things really began to change. You see, I was sexually abused throughout my childhood, and I also went through an armed home invasion. With the power of affirmations from Louise and talking to the angels, I have become the woman I once was.

I turned 50 in 2009, and in this last year I have turned my life around. A friend and I have gone into partnership and formed a "knowledge network" for women. One of our programs uses horses as mirrors of ourselves—through integrated therapy, we learn so much from them. It's empowering and a journey into who we really are. I am so excited to start other programs as well, including organic-cooking lessons, healthy living around the home, and "Dance for Freedom."

I'm so thankful to Louise for inspiring my father all those years ago to change his life, and for giving me the example to help others through my work and live my own best life.

⚲ ⚲ ⚲

The Right One for the Job
by Donna, office manager, New York

My best friend, Noelle, gave me my first Louise Hay book *(You Can Heal Your Life)* in the late '80s. For the past 20 years, Louise has been our miracle—Noelle and I have used her techniques many times over and have passed on her wonderful words of wisdom and encouragement to others.

One of my personal miracles occurred in early 1991, after I'd taken one of Louise's suggestions about writing down affirmations for myself. At the time I was in between jobs and looking for just the right one. I wrote down my affirmations on index cards and slept with them under my pillow at night. During the day I read them out loud, sometimes looking at myself in the mirror as Louise advises.

A few weeks after beginning this practice, I applied for a job at *Reader's Digest* and was subsequently called in for an interview in the Condensed Book department. The woman doing the interviewing said that she'd interviewed about 175 people for the position, yet none of them was quite right for it. Happily, she felt that *I* was. It was a unique part-time job in that it had full benefits, which I desperately needed. At the time, *Reader's Digest* had more than 20,000 employees; this was the only part-time position in the company with full benefits. I couldn't believe it! I took something else part-time in the afternoons to supplement my income; one year later, both companies offered me full-time employment. I took the one at *Reader's Digest* and worked there for ten years.

Louise, you continue to inspire me, my family, and my friends. When we talk to one another, we say, "Just go to Louise; you can heal yourself." We know that whenever we randomly open one of your books, the message we read from you is exactly what we need to know at that time. Thank you for everything!

❦ ❦ ❦

Envisioning a Brilliant Future
by Myrna, writer, Mexico

Atlanta, October 2003: As the force and name behind the *I Can Do It!* Conference, Louise Hay touched my life the minute she walked onstage, like a stream of fire. Her enthusiasm overtook me, and I scribbled furiously to capture everything she said in my journal.

Following her suggestions, I wrote down some "delicious" memories followed by a list of how I would love to live. Among other things, I envisioned a life in which I would take yoga classes and belly-dance lessons; ride my bike along the ocean; and write every day in a studio of my own, facing a big window where the moon and the sun could dance with the muses to the rhythm of the wind.

Everything Louise said that day and throughout the conference resonated within me. But one phrase really ignited my soul: "I don't know what the future holds, but I am very excited about it." Armed with that weapon of hope, the warrior in me woke up and went to work.

Taking to heart what Louise had said about how the Universe responds to our thoughts and how important it is to choose ones that are joyful and positive, I went about affirming change in my life (and my husband's, too). In May 2004, we sold all of our possessions in the United States and moved to Cozumel, Mexico, where we built a heavenly home and a business that makes our hearts sing.

I now wake up at 5:00 A.M., ride my bike through town, and am greeted by the ocean. Every other day, I practice yoga or attend belly-dance classes; every afternoon, I write for a while in the sanctuary of my studio. I sit at a checkered wooden table that faces a big window, where the moon and sun take turns to light the path for the muses to dance freely through me.

The dance has taken shape. In early 2009 my first book became available through most major electronic-distribution channels around the world—proof that the Universe does indeed respond to our thoughts.

Louise resuscitated my faith by replacing fear with hope. I now know that every experience is good for me, and that no matter what the future holds, it is exciting!

✮ ✮ ✮

What a Job Can Reflect Back to You

by Robyn, healing therapist and
clinical nurse specialist, Australia

I would say that the moment Louise L. Hay really touched my life occurred in 1999. At that time, I was working as a nurse in a psychiatric unit. During my period of employment there, aggression appeared to increase among the patients around me. When I was physically assaulted by one of them, I froze—and I knew that I needed to leave. I was quite a gentle soul, and this environment greatly affected me.

I went to my local New Age store in quite a state, wondering how my life was going to proceed. That's when I saw Louise's books *Heal Your Body* and *You Can Heal Your Life,* and the rest is history! I moved forward and never looked back. I recognized the fact that my experiences at work were encouraging me to look at my own past history and the effects that it had. Many people have been physically healed through Louise's work, and although my experience was more about my career, I knew that I needed to address some difficult things in my life in order to prevent any further physical symptoms or illness from occurring.

I'd already had many issues relating to the female reproductive area over the years, including miscarriage, ectopic pregnancies, and a stillbirth. The tragedy of losing both my daughter and my mother within a few years of each other had also taken me through a huge grieving process, which included actions that I wasn't proud of—and needless to say, the guilt and lack of self-worth I encountered were tremendous. I came to recognize that my work at the psychiatric unit was only reflecting back to me the aspects of my life that I needed to examine in order to move forward on my path.

Now, thanks to working with many of Louise's books and videos, I can honestly say that I've learned to love myself on a whole new level. Today I still work personally with Louise's affirmations, and I share them with my clients as well. That's right—I'm now working as a healing therapist and a teacher of varying healing modalities. I feel that I have the perfect job for me, in that I am surrounded by love and positive energy all the time.

I encourage my clients to have a copy of *You Can Heal Your Life* and the *I Can Do It* book-with-CD in their own personal library. I especially love *The Louise L. Hay Book Collection* (with the gift editions of *You Can Heal Your Life,* the *You Can Heal Your Life Companion Book,* and *Meditations to Heal Your Life*), as it represents the beauty of Louise's work. If the clients and students who come to me can only reap a small amount of what I've been blessed to receive, then that is all I or anyone else could ask for.

I thank you, Louise, for touching the lives of so many!

❦ ❦ ❦

The Courage to Go for It!
by Bonnie, artist, Massachusetts

I have always been an artist; in fact, being creative kept me sane in a very dysfunctional family. When I was 19 years old, I remember saying, "I am going to be an artist," but I didn't follow that path until I got a wake-up call in 1987, about five years later.

At that time, I was working for a Fortune 500 company in marketing. After an annual gynecology appointment, it was determined that I had a large cyst on my ovary. What was supposed to be a simple operation turned out to be major surgery—I was very sick and didn't even know it.

As a get-well gift, my sister bought me the book *You Can Heal Your Life,* by Louise Hay. This was the beginning of my spiritual awakening. The information in this book was foreign to me, but I was open to the concepts. I wondered why this illness had happened to me, until I read that ovaries represent the point of creation and creativity. Right then, a bell went off in my head. I'd been suppressing my creativity and denying myself something I loved doing. I had always been an artist but never had the courage to "go for it" until this experience. I realized that life is precious, and you never know when it will be your time to leave this planet. So I decided to quit my job and go back to college.

I had to sacrifice. I worked full-time at another job, went to college full-time, and made and sold jewelry at craft fairs. It took me more than seven years to complete my bachelor of fine arts degree. But I did it! And Louise helped me get where I am today.

My life just keeps getting better and better because of her teachings. Today I am a successful artist and I love the field of personal growth. Louise is with me on my nightstand, in my kitchen, and in my car; and she helped me to help myself and live a wonderful new life. I am forever grateful to Louise, and because of her I am able to say with conviction: "In the infinity of life where I am, all is perfect, whole, and complete." From the bottom of my heart, I thank her.

⚡ ⚡ ⚡

True Blessings

by Peggy, aromatherapist and teacher, United Kingdom

My life has been a series of miracles. The first one happened when I was in my 40s and living in northern Wales. I had been experiencing some marital difficulties and was feeling deeply unhappy. After reading Louise Hay's book *You Can Heal Your Life*, I decided to record a creative visualization and some affirmations on a tape to use for myself. After completing the recording, I visited my daughter who lived in a neighboring village. When I arrived, she let me know that she was moving and offered me the opportunity to live in her current home for a few weeks to think about my situation. While living there, I listened to my tape recording over and over, and I experienced heightened auditory and visual, as well as telepathic, abilities. This completely changed my life. Over the following years, I returned to education, eventually qualifying as an aromatherapist and counselor.

I'd decided to train as a Louise Hay teacher, but I was in a car accident and arrived at the course with severe back pain. Nevertheless, I was surrounded by so many positive and lovely people that I quickly forgot about my pain. Over the course of three days, we learned to use Louise's affirmations and create our own, and then we were instructed to put her teachings into practice as well as train others to use them. By the third day, I was well enough to dance with my fellow students!

When the course was over, I felt inspired to take on the challenge of running several aromatherapy-massage weekend courses. I shared the skills, affirmations, and songs I'd learned at my Louise Hay training course with my massage students. This enabled them to gain confidence in working with comparative strangers in such an intimate setting. I can truly say that now, in my late 60s, I have the career of my dreams.

Here's an interesting postscript: I live in southern Spain these days. Soon after arriving here, I saw the most amazing house advertised for rent; unfortunately, by the time I managed to see it, it had been sold. Many times I walked up there to admire the superb views from the neighboring church square, and I continually visualized what it would be like to live in a house just like that. Eventually I met the new owners of the house, and we became good friends. One year later, I'm now renting this home, as the proprietors had to move back to the U.K.

I continue to be inspired by Louise's books, recordings, and DVDs; and I am enjoying many more wondrous experiences. I feel truly blessed.

ᴋ ᴋ ᴋ

I'm Now a Free Woman
by Lisa, personal assistant, Ohio

My life has changed dramatically this past year, and I believe that Louise Hay's books and teachings were the catalysts that inspired that change.

For 15 years I'd been living in a loveless and verbally abusive marriage, and I believed that I had no way out. Then I read Louise's book *You Can Heal Your Life* two years ago, and it was as if someone had opened a door I never knew existed. Everything became clearer to me, and my intentions for my life grew more focused and sharper in clarity. When I watched the movie version of the book, it confirmed my newfound belief that I had the power within me to make my life what I wanted it to be. I could create a new life for myself and my children, one that was filled with happiness and peace.

I began to meditate daily on my intentions. I'd visualize how I wanted my life to be, and then I'd say my affirmations out loud. The first affirmation had to do with leaving my marriage peacefully; the second had to do with a job. I was a stay-at-home mom with three children, and my husband controlled the money. I knew that I needed to have well-paying employment in order for my life to transition smoothly.

When I said my affirmations, I ended them with "I receive it now." I found that when I said those words out loud, my heart felt lighter, as if the pressing worry I carried within me eased and the Universe itself took it away.

I am so happy and grateful to report that my marriage is ending in a civil way, and I've just secured a fantastic job. In this economy, landing a job like this is a miracle in and of itself. My family and friends are astounded, and I smile, knowing that the Universe partnered with me on this.

Throughout this process, I continually held gratitude as the central theme of my affirmations, and I offered my words up as prayers to Spirit and my guides. They've proven so faithful to me.

Louise, thank you for your teachings; you're an inspiration to me. Because of you, I'm now a free woman with a wonderful job and an even better life.

ﾉﾟ ﾉﾟ ﾉﾟ

Louise's Work . . . and Mine
by Mary Margarette, chief executive officer, Australia

In 1994 I was hospitalized with severe back pain. I was treated with injections for the pain and placed in traction, yet doctors weren't able to make a diagnosis.

As I was going through all of this, my sister called me and asked where the pain was located. When I said it was from my waist down, she replied, "You're suffering with guilt and have a fear of money."

My marriage had ended after 20 years, and I was now living in a small apartment with very little furniture. I had no money and was dealing with a new business that was struggling. Shocked by what my sister said, I asked, "How did you know that?"

"It's in the book *You Can Heal Your Life,*" she explained.

I had a friend go buy the book for me, and I read most of it right away. I was out of the hospital the following day (pain free) and became a sponge for Louise's words. Positive affirmations were my life, and I lived and breathed Louise's work.

In 1997, I stumbled upon a brochure about a "Love Yourself, Heal Your Life" training course in San Diego, California. Still working hard to build my business, I was determined to attend. Following the course, I returned home to Australia to conduct many of these training courses on weekends over the next four years while continuing to build my business.

I completed my doctorate in psychology and am now the chief executive officer of my own multimillion-dollar private nursing service. In 2007 I established a learning institution where we teach many courses, including personal development—and incorporating Louise's work. I share Louise's messages with all of my administration staff, providing them with affirmations at our monthly meetings. Both my sons and their partners also work with me and share my love of Louise and what she does.

My back pain has never returned; today, I am healthy, happy, and wealthy. I'm proud to say that I continue Louise's work, which has become my own as well.

Tapping into My Inner Strength

by Montie, interior designer, Missouri

Fifteen years ago, I was a young widow with two teenage children. My husband had died suddenly of a massive heart attack—in one breath, my world turned upside down. Although I knew nothing of his business, I foolishly thought I would be eased through the estate-settlement process. Things turned ugly very quickly. It became apparent that I was going to have to pull myself together and wear three hats. The first was that of a smart businesswoman (even though I had no experience), the second was that of an attentive and loving mother to two wonderful but devastated children, and the third was my grieving hat.

I have always been a spiritual person, but that wasn't helping me now. Several people in my husband's company were working against me, and my life seemed to be a mess. One day, after yet another night of sobbing myself to sleep, I was standing in front of the self-help section of my local bookstore, browsing for a miracle. As I pulled a volume from the shelf, one next to it fell directly on my foot. I picked it up, thinking that this must be the one I needed. It was *You Can Heal Your Life.*

After buying Louise's book and poring over it several times, I realized that it was important to choose thoughts that would empower me. It wasn't in my best interest to think negatively or act like a victim; it was time to tap into my inner strength. The book gave me such hope, and it started to wash away most of my fears. When I couldn't sleep at night, instead of having anxiety attacks or dissolving into tears, I now repeated affirmations and visualized how I wanted the next day to go. Every day, things started changing in a positive way. It was magical, and I have Louise Hay to thank.

I ended up taking charge of my life by setting up an office, learning how to invest, and starting my own company—which I have owned for the last 11 years. I guess I *am* a businesswoman after all! I married a wonderful man, who is my partner in life as well as my partner in spiritual discovery, and my children are happy and successful in their own lives and careers.

Louise changed my life, and as I continue on my journey, I feel so blessed to be able to pass along her words of wisdom and books to friends and family. (By the way, my husband, daughter, and I actually met Louise . . . what a thrill! I promised her that I would share my story with the world, and I'm so grateful for the opportunity to do so.)

𝓴 𝓴 𝓴

Luck, or Louise?
by Mary Kate, writer, Ireland

In 2005 I was unhappy, more overweight than I had ever been, in a bad relationship, and finding it hard to support myself. Feeling lost, I couldn't face the struggle of the remaining 40 or 50 years of my life. I decided to go on a health retreat, yet when I arrived I discovered that I, a voracious reader, had forgotten to pack a book for the first time in my life. Luckily, the retreat had a library, and *You Can Heal Your Life* caught my eye. I took it to bed and started to read. When I finished it the next day, I read it again. As I did, it felt like a bell was ringing inside of me. This was the help I'd been seeking.

That autumn, I attended several Louise Hay workshops run by an inspiring teacher. When I returned, my relationship ended; although there was sadness, I was ready for the future. I'd been so unhappy for years, and now I was happy again because I finally understood the truth about what it meant to choose my thoughts. Even though the outward manifestations were small at that time, my loved ones still commented on my transformation. The bigger manifestations were on their way, however.

I made it a habit to put up Louise's affirmation cards on the mirror in my home, bless myself in the mirror as often as I remembered, and listen to her *Morning and Evening Meditations* CD every day. It wasn't long before miracles fell into my life. For example, I started the year temping for minimum wage and ended by earning an unprecedented amount of money, considerably above the national average. I won a place in a terrific training course, began to pursue my master's degree, and attracted a big contract. I took myself on a honeymoon to Venice to celebrate my 40th birthday, and friends joined me there for a magical weekend. Wonderful people started to come into my life, including a very valuable mentor and friend who has helped my career enormously. People started to think it was a joke how lucky I'd suddenly become.

Today I continue to be offered great opportunities and travel all over the globe with my work, which I love passionately. I take better care of my physical self now that I like myself; and my body is stronger, lighter, and more toned. My relationships are better than ever, and although my life is not perfect (and *I* am certainly not perfect), I live in a state of appreciation most of the time. My beloved father died unexpectedly in late 2006, for instance, and although I miss him terribly, I coped with his loss by practicing gratitude and appreciation for all he ever was and had given me before he passed.

Rewards, big and small, keep pouring into my life. Louise is with me in many moments of my day, especially as I wake up and go to sleep. Her work didn't just heal my life; it *saved* my life. My gratitude to her is inexpressible.

✕ ✕ ✕

Always Have Faith in the Power of Affirmations
by Devon, copywriter, California

Back in 1993, my friend Alexa and I were working together at an ad agency, but we were both miserable. There were about 30 people (mostly gossipy women) packed into an office space as big as a large lunchroom, and there was a lot of negative energy.

Every day during our lunch hour, Alexa and I would walk around the neighborhood and say affirmations. We were both fans of Louise Hay, so we would adapt her positive thoughts to our situation and repeat statements like the following each afternoon: *We work together at a company we love. We are paid well for what we do, and our income is constantly increasing. We have a wonderful relationship with our co-workers.* And so on . . .

Anyway, since at that time we lived about 45 miles apart, we thought it pretty unlikely that we'd both end up working at the same place again.

However, always have faith in the power of affirmations. . . .

That firm we were working for laid off the entire staff, so Alexa and I scattered. I went to work at another ad agency as a copywriter (but wasn't enjoying it), and Alexa went back to school.

Out of the blue, I got a call from a company I'd worked at briefly four years earlier. At that time, the company was located midway between where Alexa and I lived—and another friend of mine was doing the hiring. He said that the company wanted to hire an art director, and did I know anyone. I immediately thought of Alexa. To make a long story short, she was hired. A few weeks later, I got another call inquiring if *I* would like to return to this company as a copywriter. Of course I said yes!

So . . . Alexa and I did end up working together at a company we love, due in no small part to our admiration for Louise and the affirmations we shared.

And we've now been here for . . . *16 happy years!*

Doing the Work with Louise

Every one of us is where we are today because of the thinking patterns we have chosen. The people and "problems" around us are only reflecting what we believe we deserve.

If all of your thoughts regarding work are negative, how do you expect to create a happy working environment? Bless your current position (whether you have a job or not) and understand that wherever you are, it is a stepping-stone on the path of the rest of your life. Focus your mind on the career and working environment you want by doing the exercises below. Write your answers on a separate piece of paper or in your journal.

Center Yourself

Before you begin, take a moment to center yourself. Place your right hand over your lower stomach area. Think of this area as the center of your being. Breathe. Look into a mirror and say three times: *"I am willing to release the need to be so unhappy at work."* Each time, say it a little differently. What you want to do is increase your commitment to change.

Your Work Life

Let's explore your thoughts regarding your job:

1. Do you work in a pleasant environment?
2. What would you like to change about your current job?
3. What would you change about your employer?
4. Do you feel worthy of having a good job?
5. What do you fear most about work?
6. What are you "getting" from this belief?

Describe the People in Your Work Environment

Now, how do you feel about the people you currently work with? Use ten adjectives to describe your:

- Boss
- Co-workers
- Clients or customers

Think about the Economy

Many people worry about the economy and believe they will either earn or lose money due to the economic situation at present. However, the economy is always moving up and down. So, it doesn't matter what is happening "out there," or what others do to change the economy. No matter what is happening in the world, it only matters what you believe about yourself.

Now, think about what your perfect job would be. Release any fears related to the economy, and really dream big. Take a moment to see yourself in the job. Visualize yourself in the environment, see your co-workers, and feel what it would be like to do work that's completely fulfilling—while you earn a good salary. Hold that vision for yourself, and know that it has been fulfilled in your consciousness.

Blessing with Love

Blessing with love is a powerful tool. Start using it now by sending love and blessings ahead of you before you arrive at your place of employment. Bless every person, place, or thing there with love. If you have a problem with a co-worker, a boss, a supplier, or even the temperature in the building, bless it with love. Affirm that you and the person or situation are in agreement and in perfect harmony.

Select an affirmation below or create your own that fits an issue in your workplace, and repeat it over and over. Every time the person or situation comes to mind, repeat the affirmation. Eliminate the negative energy in your mind regarding this issue. You can, just by thinking, change the experience.

Affirmations

I am always happy at work. My career is filled with joy, laughter, and abundance.

My work allows me to express my creativity freely. I earn good money doing what I love.

I am capable and competent and in the perfect place.

I go beyond my parents' income level.

I always work for the most wonderful bosses, who treat me with love and respect.

There are plenty of customers for my services.

I enjoy the work I do and the people I work with.

I create peace in my mind, and my work environment reflects this.

My work is recognized by everyone.

I am deeply fulfilled by all that I do.

My income is constantly increasing, regardless of the economy.

Everything I touch is a success.

I am in perfect harmony with my work environment and everyone in it.

My boss is generous and easy to work for.

Everybody at work appreciates me.

I am open and receptive to new avenues of income.

I turn every experience into an opportunity.

I now accept a wonderful, fulfilling career.

I am totally open and receptive to an amazing new position that uses all my talents and abilities.

New doors are opening all the time.

Treatment for Career Challenges

My unique creative talents and abilities flow through me and are expressed in deeply satisfying ways. There are people out there who are always looking for my services. I am always in demand and can pick and choose what I want to do. I earn good money doing what satisfies me. My work is a joy and a pleasure. All is well in my world.

Chapter Six

Working with Children and Family Issues

Patterns of belief get passed down through families because children are influenced by the mental atmosphere of the people around them. So whatever our parents believed about things such as prosperity, health, guilt, and love, we usually accepted. Often, we continue to carry these patterns around as adults.

Please do not see this as an excuse to resent your parents and blame your past for all your problems. That just keeps you stuck in a victim mentality. You then pass on the same beliefs that are making you unhappy to your children, and your children's children. You have the opportunity to break the cycle right now by forgiving and letting go of the past. When you create harmony within yourself, you create harmony throughout your family.

The following stories depict some of the many different ways in which children and family issues have been healed or transformed.

Helping Kids out of the Darkness
by Ronald and Miguel, foster parents, Vermont

We are a gay couple and foster parents, taking in teenagers who have failed in multiple placements. When the kids come to us, they're usually filled with negative thoughts and a desire to control everything and everyone in their environment, which always leads to unhappiness. Every one of these boys and girls has been spiritually wounded, so we greatly appreciate the help that Louise Hay has been to us in helping these young people heal themselves.

Every day we spread out Louise's *Power Thought Cards,* and we each pick one to read as our message of the day. When we go on long trips, we play Louise's audiotapes in the car to give the teens positive messages. And when we show them the DVD of *You Can Heal Your Life, the movie,* they often have tears streaming down their cheeks and feel that this film is speaking directly to them. Louise's messages help reinforce our message to these kids that they are good, worthwhile people who deserve respect and dignity, and that they can attract good things into their lives with a positive attitude.

We've both seen that when we're working to help these young men and women heal themselves, we're also healing parts of *ourselves* that we never even knew needed to be healed. By helping the kids learn how to take responsibility for their own happiness, we clarified the same message for ourselves. And by helping them learn to forgive what was done to them by their parents, we remembered to forgive people in our own lives.

Louise's work has helped make all of this much easier than it would have been otherwise. She is a blessing for our family, and we deeply appreciate her and her work. I hope that she knows how many people she has touched with her inspiration, and how many lives are now lived in light instead of darkness.

❦ ❦ ❦

Affirmations Work for Children, Too!
by Carla, Internet-marketing specialist, Texas

When my daughter, Haley, was in kindergarten, she received "red marks" for being too chatty several times a week. I'd tell her,

"Baby, you've got to pay attention and quit talking," but that didn't change anything. In first grade, we had the same issue. I used a different approach and threatened to take things away from her, but that didn't really work either.

When Haley started second grade, I was introduced to Louise Hay. I'd already been a fan of *The Secret,* Wayne Dyer, and Esther Hicks; however, *You Can Heal Your Life* removed the blinders from my eyes.

Haley began school as her usual self. After receiving "too chatty" comments for the first nine weeks, I spoke to her teacher. She told me that my daughter was just social and that I shouldn't worry. She said that Haley was well liked by her classmates and wasn't being disruptive—she was just responding to those attempting to get her attention.

Just like my daughter, I am also very social and didn't want to scold her for being who I want her to be. Therefore, I came up with a positive affirmation for her, which we repeated constantly: *I am a good listener.* I figured that if she was thinking about being a good listener, she wouldn't be able to talk and listen at the same time. It worked—Haley didn't receive any red marks for the rest of the school year. She's also learned to share her positive thoughts with her friends and has made me very proud.

I've just started a new affirmation for my daughter. In the first grade, she was labeled a "slow reader." Teachers actually said those words to her. I recently received a letter from one of them, stating that Haley would be getting additional help for her reading problem. I responded to the teacher by explaining the approach I was going to take with Haley. As I informed her, "I firmly believe you become what you think. After being told that many times over the years, Haley knows this to be true. The method I'm using to help her in school has been very effective for us. Call me crazy if you'd like, but it works for Haley and me. Therefore, the positive affirmation we've created is: *I understand everything I read.*"

I have printed this latest affirmation on paper and stickers and have placed them everywhere in our home—even inside the refrigerator. I've also affixed stickers to every notebook and folder

Haley brings home from school. It's only been five days, yet my daughter is already expressing more confidence in her reading.

Thank you, Louise Hay. You are wonderful.

❈ ❈ ❈

An "Impossible Dream" Comes True
by Connie, currently job hunting, Florida

It was 1990 and I'd been married for ten years and longed to have children. To me, it wasn't a driving desire to "have my own," because I'd been adopted. My adoptive mom was herself adopted, and even my birth mom had been adopted. Although having a biological child would have been a blessing, passing on my DNA was nothing special. I simply wanted a child to love. However, my husband and I experienced several setbacks in our adoption efforts and felt jinxed. By age 40, I was sure that my motherhood clock had run out. Then I started reading *You Can Heal Your Life,* by Louise Hay.

I have phobias about crossing bridges, so imagine my family members' surprise when I flew to Romania alone, without knowing a single person there. But Louise Hay had helped me realize my destiny, and I instinctively knew a child was waiting for me in that country. I listened to one of Louise's cassettes nightly. As I closed my eyes each evening in the tiny apartment I shared with people who spoke no English, it was her voice that helped me face danger and despair.

Few people can imagine what I saw during the day: babies dying of AIDS; street children begging for food; filthy, freezing, uninhabitable orphanages for disabled kids; soldiers in tanks facing unarmed demonstrators seeking freedom. I realized how much we in the "civilized world" take for granted. But imagine my joy when I did find the baby who was waiting for me . . . and then I went back and did it all again a couple years later.

Today, the two Romanian-born children my husband and I adopted are adults. Our son overcame many challenges, such as "failure to thrive" and severe deprivation. In the seventh grade, so-called experts said that he was too brain damaged to ever learn to read or earn a high-school diploma. Well, he succeeded beyond their expectations: he took honors English, honors physics, and honors algebra 2 his senior year, and not only did he graduate, but he earned a partial college scholarship as well. He has chosen to serve in the military before continuing his education. Our daughter also faced many challenges, but she now works two jobs while attending college full-time and earns a 3.8 grade point average.

I thank Louise for encouraging me. Her words made it possible for two kids to have a home in a place where many dreams come true: Orlando, Florida. Helping people heal the past and make impossible dreams come true is what Louise does best, which I can certainly attest to.

ᴋ ᴋ ᴋ

A Family's Leap of Faith
by Nancy, English as a second
language (ESL) instructor, Germany

Learning how to create health, happiness, and life satisfaction has been the miracle for our whole family—and we credit it all to Louise Hay. Shortly after my second son was born, I became ill with a variety of viruses and bacterial infections. It seemed that I'd finally be starting to get my strength back when I'd develop another infection or get another cold, or I'd suffer breakouts all over my face and chest. During this time I continued to work part-time at two different jobs while my husband worked nights. We rarely saw each other and felt exhausted all the time, yet we thought we had things under control.

When I finally got tired of being sick all the time, I went to an alternative practitioner for advice. Among other things, I was told about Louise's book *Heal Your Body,* which then led me to *You Can Heal Your Life.* Luckily, both my husband and I were "open" to these books—he read them in German, his native language, and

I read them in English. Louise's ideas made sense to us, and we started putting them into practice. One of the first affirmations we tried was to help our eldest son with a cough that seemed to continually plague him at night. My husband spent one night lying next to our boy, cuddling him and repeating a simple version of Louise's phrases. It was amazingly easy, and it worked: our son fell into a peaceful sleep, and the cough simply disappeared, never to return again.

After that, our life took on a lot of changes. My husband and I did a great deal of soul-searching, meditating, and forgiving. Within about a six-month period, I was feeling healthier; my husband was working in a new job that fit our family schedule better; and we both looked at life with more compassion, understanding, patience, and love. Louise's ideas have also become a large part of our children's upbringing. I made each one his own tape with personal affirmations to fit each age and personality; although I made these tapes years ago, the kids often still listen to them before going to sleep at night. We hear Louise's ideas come out of their mouths when they say, "My affirmation is: *I now do better in school,*" or "I changed my thoughts when [a situation] wasn't working the right way."

There are always new challenges to face, but my whole family feels better equipped to face them as a result of all we've learned from Louise. Our choice to adapt her beliefs to our lives was a leap of faith that has truly given us a miracle. We love her and can't thank her enough.

❧ ❧ ❧

My Two Mothers
by Carolyn, director of a nonprofit
holistic-learning center, Virginia

I grew up in a very volatile, abusive home with two alcoholic parents. After my father committed suicide at age 42, I naïvely thought that since he was gone, my mother's drinking would probably disappear as well. Alas, she just drank more. As the eldest child in the family, I took on even more responsibilities for both my mother and brother.

Years later, after moving out and moving on with my life, Mom would often call me in a drunken stupor to tell me that she was sticking her head in the gas oven. I still wanted happiness for her, but I realized that no one could really bring her joy except *her*. I told her that she could go the oven route, or she could come to where I was and let me help her get her life back together. She chose the latter, ultimately ending up in a halfway house for alcoholic women, where she remained sober in their care for a year. She managed to "do her time," but our relationship suffered because of the bitterness she inflicted on me.

I remember a phone conversation with my mother that angered me so much I literally threw my hands up into the air and asked God to please help me. The very next day I was gifted with a Louise Hay video—and upon watching it, I knew she was my teacher. After attending two of her ten-day intensives in California, I came home to start a "healing circle" that met weekly for six years. I passed on Louise's philosophy of life to hundreds of people during that time, and it was amazing.

I followed Louise around, even to Holland and Australia, taking folks with me to hear her speak and showcase other great motivational authors. The healing circle then morphed into a nonprofit organization that I founded and preside over. Louise and I actually became friends, and I've had the opportunity to share this amazing woman and her story with countless men and women who have chosen to change their lives.

My own life and attitude were transformed because I chose to apply Louise's simple philosophies. To that end, my mother and I finally made real peace with each other a few years before her passing, which was powerfully healing for us both. I've come to truly know, love, understand, and forgive both my parents, and I see the wonderful lessons they came here to teach me.

I've always felt like I've been blessed with two mothers: the one who showed me the lessons I was brought here to learn, and the other who taught me how to heal myself. God bless you, Mom! And God bless you, Louise! Thank you for everything!

⚹ ⚹ ⚹

The Miracle of Conception
by Maria, communications worker, Mexico

I am a very happy and fortunate person. I found out about Louise Hay around 2001, and I discovered a whole new way of living, as well as many powerful tools. Even though I'd previously learned about metaphysics and the power of affirmations through other authors, I really resonated with Louise's philosophy. I used many affirmations from Louise's books and even started a program of affirmations for my little girl, Renata, who was born in 2000.

I had a tough time getting pregnant again. In 2004, after six months of trying, my husband and I decided to see a doctor, who gave us hormonal therapy. We also tried three artificial inseminations, but nothing happened. I was told that I needed to have exploratory surgery to make sure I wouldn't have uterine adhesions. I agreed to have this procedure; after putting me under general anesthesia and poking three holes in me, the doctors said I was healthy. We tried a fourth insemination, and again, nothing happened.

In December 2006, I quit trying. I told myself, *For years I've been creating everything I want or need in my life, but now I'm not being able to do so. God is sending me a clear message: I should stop and explore what's going on inside me. I need to know how I created this problem.*

By then I'd already started therapy in an attempt to "dig deep" inside me. In January 2007 I attended the "Miracle Cure" workshop, which was mostly a meditation and mental-exercise program. This is where I found out about Louise's *Meditations for Personal Healing* CD. I live in Monterrey, Mexico, and we don't have much of Louise's material around here; luckily, I was able to find my own copy of the CD through the Internet.

I practiced what was on this CD for two months. I tried to remain in the flow. I made a list of affirmations, which I took from Louise's book *You Can Heal Your Life*. I told myself that if Renata was the only child I was to have, that would be just fine. But on March 21, 2007, I found out I was pregnant—Rodrigo was born on November 11 and is a very happy little man. I feel so very blessed.

I'm absolutely sure that my affirmations and meditations healed whatever was wrong with me. I am so convinced that Louise's philosophy works that I want to share it everywhere and with everyone, and I plan to get the Louise Hay Leader Training certificate this year.

⫧ ⫧ ⫧

A Daughter Finally Learns to Forgive
by Lynn, high-school teacher, California

I have had issues with my mother forever. She was critical, controlling, and overprotective; consequently, I became fearful of everything. I tried a few times to break away from her, even moving out of the country, but I always came back looking for her approval. I never got it, nor did I ever get her support. Whenever I went to her with a problem while I was growing up, she'd take the other side and say that she was "playing devil's advocate." I continually felt that something was wrong with me because I was feeling the way I did or thought the things I did.

I tried to tell myself that my mother was doing the best she could, but I grew to resent her (and myself) because I just couldn't tell her how I felt. Friends would urge me to confront her, but I never could. I'd just get quiet as she talked and wait for her to stop. Then I went on to marry a man who treated me the same way. I didn't count in the marriage—he wasn't interested in how I felt about things, but wanted a wife who went along with what he wanted. Whenever I did manage to speak up, he'd pull away even more. Yet I stayed with him for 23 years!

While going through treatment for breast cancer, a friend gave me books by Dr. Bernie Siegel and Louise Hay. They opened up a world I never knew existed before, and I just read and read. Finally, I was able to get the strength to leave my husband. I'd repeat the affirmations that Louise suggested anytime I felt scared or inadequate; and even though I was terrified, I was amazed to find out that I could take care of myself and my son quite well.

I found a meditation CD that Louise made to help you forgive those in your life you have issues with. I listened to it a few times before I was actually able to forgive my mother. I couldn't believe it, but after listening to Louise and following her instructions, I felt calm and peaceful. I wasn't angry anymore. After that, I was able to speak up to my mother when I needed to, and surprisingly, she listened. We actually became closer, and she really began to respect me and tell me so. She recently passed, and I was truly able to grieve for her. I am so grateful to Louise because I can't imagine living the rest of my life feeling guilty for not forgiving my mother and never being able to tell her I loved her.

✕ ✕ ✕

Transforming My Life . . . and Saving My Son's
by Michele, senior underwriter, Wisconsin

It is an honor to have the opportunity to write about a woman whom I consider to be "the" worldwide healer, thanks to her wise and profound words that transform countless lives. I believe that she was handpicked to teach God's healing grace.

Let me start by explaining how Louise Hay came into my life. My body had a physical breakdown, and after seeking medical assistance from numerous doctors (who did nothing), I pleaded with the heavens above to show me how to heal my body. I was at my most desperate state when *You Can Heal Your Life* was introduced to me. What occurred as I read this life-altering book was miraculous. Louise was the "doctor" I needed, and she's gone on to become a mentor for me on how to truly see, feel, and experience life. What

I learned through higher education is nothing compared to the knowledge I've received through Louise's miraculous teachings. Her philosophy must be a requirement class in schools today. Imagine if children were raised with her life-loving message!

How did Louise touch my soul and enable me to transform my life into healthy wonders? Well, her wisdom taught me the power of the present moment. I had no understanding of this power until Louise showed me the way. These words enlightened my thinking power: *It's only a thought, and a thought can be changed.* I discovered how to love and approve of myself exactly as I am. I transformed my world through the daily use of mirror affirmations. I forgave life, people, and circumstances; and I was set free.

After routinely applying Louise's lessons and affirmations numerous times, it became a way of life. The gift of self-love I learned not only transformed me, it saved my son's life as well. As I applied Louise's way of thinking to heal myself, little did I know that her wisdom was preparing me for my biggest challenge.

Toward the end of my personal healing pathway, my son was diagnosed as "terminally ill" with numerous brain tumors. The old Michele would not have known how to heal him; the life-awakened Michele knew that there was a gift within this trauma, and the means to save his life would be shown to me. Through innovative chemotherapy medications and Louise's holistic approach, I was able to guide my son to wellness with pure love, faith, and constant mirror affirmations.

My deepest gratitude and thankfulness to you, Louise, today and always. May you continue to bless the universe with your loving presence for years to come.

Miracle of the Heart
by Sampoorna, psychologist and therapist, India

In my line of work, I hear about personal transformation all the time. While "people stories" are certainly inspiring, this one is different. Here, Louise Hay creates a miracle for a dog in India.

Eleven-year-old Manav badly wanted a pup. After months of persuasion, his parents reluctantly conceded, and an Irish setter named Flurry entered their home. A year later, Manav's mother, Geetha, came to me in a state of distress because Flurry was very ill and would need to be put to sleep right away. Manav was so distraught that he stayed home from school to spend as much time as possible with Flurry, taking pictures on his mother's cell phone to help keep his beloved friend in his memory.

Geetha and her husband, Prakash, were familiar with Louise Hay's work through my "Love Yourself, Heal Your Life" workshop. For two full days prior to making the painful decision about Flurry, Geetha had been repeatedly playing Louise's *Stress-Free* CD in her bedroom, where Flurry was lying immobilized. She was bombarding him with affirmations without a break, and the family was flooding the dog with love. When Geetha and I spoke, she decided to wait a few more days before euthanizing Flurry. After all, what if he recovered? So Louise's voice continued to speak to the animal throughout the entire stressful period.

Needless to say, the story has a happy ending. It wasn't long before the immobilized Flurry started to move and then heal. As soon as he began eating again, he recovered at tremendous speed. Today the dog thrives, healthfully prancing around, full of energy, and completely integrated into his loving family. And they are all grateful for this bond.

After Flurry recovered, Geetha noticed the photographs her son had taken on her cell phone. Manav had taken four pictures of his dog in the very same position, consecutively—and Geetha noticed that one of them had the backdrop of a heart of light. Since it was only on one of the pictures, this proved that the heart was not some reflection. Louise's voice and her messages of love permeated through all barriers of race and language to create healing and life for Flurry. That the light shone in the same shape as Louise's own heart symbol is significant.

Oh, the miracle of love!

❧ ❧ ❧

Little Changes, Big Impact
by Terrie, family child-care provider, California

I have been a family child-care provider working with Head Start for many years, and my day-to-day experiences have been so enriching and life-changing.

I've been to many training seminars on how to work with children, but one in particular changed my life. I was introduced to the teachings of Louise Hay and learned how much impact positive thinking and speaking can have on children. I began to say things to the kids like, "You should be so proud of yourself" instead of "I am so proud of you," and telling them yes more often.

I found that just saying a child's first and last name in a positive way can be an especially powerful instrument of change. Kids are so used to hearing "Michael Smith, you get over here this instant!" that statements like "I'm really glad you're here today, Michael Smith" have a profound effect, both on the children and myself. I've heard many parents over the years remark that these seemingly small things changed their kids' way of thinking. It is so rewarding to see what just being positive can do for people of all ages.

Louise, I've worked all of my life to protect children, so I truly appreciate all your great work!

❧ ❧ ❧

My Real Life
by Chantale, job-seeker, Canada

The first time I came across *You Can Heal Your Life* was during my early teenage years. I remember reading the book with a smile on my face, thinking, *Okay now, this is some woo-woo, dance-around-the-fire kind of thing.*

A few years passed and I found myself with only one choice to make: live or kill myself. I arrived at this juncture as the result of very heavy family issues. To make a long story short, my father left when I was four, and my mother and I went to live with my grandmother, who liked to tell me that I was a worthless failure. My mom never took my side because she didn't want to raise a kid alone. She always looked the other way whenever my grandmother abused me. Then Prince Charming came into my mother's life and promised to take care of us. This "savior" turned out to be sexually obsessed, worked 24/7, and loved red wine; and his daughter went into a jealous rampage over me for years. Again, my mother looked the other way.

It was at this point that Louise Hay came across my path again, and this time I was ready to hear what she had to say. Her positive affirmations really struck a chord with me, and I post them everywhere. I'm also a huge fan of her mirror work, which has helped to heal much in my life. Today I feel strong, clean, at peace, and calm—and I finally have some self-respect and self-esteem.

I've never had a deadly disease and I've never lost anyone, so how can this be a miracle? Well, considering where I was not so long ago, it's clear that without Louise, I would be dead by now. She gave me back my real life, and I am so grateful.

✹ ✹ ✹

New Thought Patterns for Mother and Daughter
by Barbara, writer, Florida

She was only seven, yet earaches plagued her nightly sleep. Each time I called my daughter, I heard another tale of how my granddaughter had been screaming during the night. *This just isn't normal,* I thought. My first reaction was to reach for my now-worn copy of Louise Hay's *You Can Heal Your Life.* On page 166 I found the answer. I nodded as I read what Louise had written and gave thanks. It turns out that anger is the probable cause of earaches, and that anger can stem from "too much turmoil" or "parents arguing."

How could Louise possibly know? She'd hit the nail right on the head. My daughter and son-in-law had been fighting for years, but she didn't want a divorce. "It would hurt the children," she kept telling me. "I just feel it is better they have a mother and father. I hated that you and Dad divorced."

I called my daughter right away, telling her, "I have the greatest news. Trust me, I know what will work." I related what I'd just read in *You Can Heal Your Life*. I emphasized the importance of her sitting with my granddaughter before going to sleep each night, and having her repeat the "new thought pattern" Louise suggested, right after her nightly prayer.

Needless to say, I called every morning for a week to encourage her (and yes, I admit, to make certain that Louise's words were being used). I breathed a sigh of relief when I heard that my granddaughter was falling asleep repeating her new thought pattern, and she was saying it when she woke up as well.

After that first week, I quit my morning "checkup calls," secure that Louise's technique was working. But then after three weeks had passed, I thought, *Hmm . . . I haven't heard about any earaches lately. I better see what's going on.*

Imagine my delight when my daughter told me, "Mom, it's a miracle. She hasn't had an earache for weeks. I didn't realize that our fighting was hurting our little girl so much. You'll be pleased to know that I now have my very own copy of *You Can Heal Your Life*. Oh, and you'll love this. I stubbed my toe the other day and told myself, *There's a message here*. I picked up the book and read about toes on page 204. Trust me, my morning and evening mantra is now: *All details take care of themselves.*

"Thanks, Mom. I love you, and I love Louise."

彡 彡 彡

The Power of Forgiving and Finally Forgetting
by Carmen, Realtor, California

My mother was diagnosed with lymphoma in March 2008. She declined rapidly and lost about 30 pounds within five months. I purchased *You Can Heal Your Life* for her; when she proved to be too weak to read it on her own, I read it aloud to her. Mom had had a rough life, and I kept reminding her that any pain and resentment she'd held in her heart throughout her life's journey was something she *had* to release *here* and *now*. I stressed the importance of her letting go of her past pain even as I worked hard to lift her spirits.

Six months later, hospice was ordered—the treatment that had been recommended for Mom had severe side effects, and the rest of the family and I decided not to put this 82-year-old woman through that misery. We didn't give up on her, though, and continued to feed her many positive thoughts and lots of laughter. All of this paid off, as she is now singing and dancing and is back to her normal self.

Mom came into my bedroom one day and said, "You know what, I have finally forgiven all of the wrong and let it go. I feel great about everything and don't even think about those bad times anymore." This was a big deal, since she always used to tell me, "I forgive, but I can't ever forget." I liked to remind her that if she couldn't forget, then she couldn't truly forgive. Well, she finally forgot!

As I write this, it is now ten months after my mother's diagnosis. What we all thought would be a grim New Year has begun with a bright outlook. Mom is happy again and at peace.

Louise, I can't tell you how important you've been to my mother's healing—I know that she was very inspired by how you yourself overcame cancer. Thank you for your wonderful words, which hold all the truth we need to survive whatever life brings to us. My family and I are having wonderful quality time with Mom . . . thanks to you!

ⱴ ⱴ ⱴ

From Hopelessness to Miracles
by Dixie, advocate for children and the disabled,
writer, and mother of eight, Massachusetts

The one thing I've learned through Louise Hay's writings is this: if people try to respond to life's obstacles with optimistic thoughts and positive affirmations, then these so-called obstacles can ultimately bring peace, healing, and hope.

I found this to be true back in 2001, when my 13-year-old son, Paul, was struck by an SUV. He was given last rites and remained in a coma for eight weeks. When his eyes finally did open, Paul remained hospitalized for months as he relearned how to walk, talk, and perform the basics of life again. His traumatic brain injury changed his life and that of his seven siblings forever.

Our family could have reacted with anger, helplessness, and fear; instead, we chose to live by Louise's words. We didn't give in to our hopelessness but began thinking (and living!) positively, which ultimately led to hope. Paul healed enough to no longer need his wheelchair and then his walker—eventually, he was able to take the steps that doctors had deemed impossible and even walked independently to the podium to receive his high-school diploma.

Louise reminds us that we can change our attitude about life's negatives and unforeseen circumstances by reacting, thinking, and choosing to give back to the universe in positive ways every moment of the day. That's why when Paul was diagnosed with leukemia four years after his traumatic brain injury, my family once again got into the positive-thinking pattern. We put on the armor of faith, perseverance, and determination—and cloaked it with a sense of humor and a lot of love—to help our family through our next battle. By reading Louise's books and putting her way of living and thinking into action, we were able to deal with the situation. Thankfully, one of Paul's siblings was a positive match for a bone-marrow transplant. Although my son underwent more years of hospitalizations, isolation, and cancer treatments, he and our family ultimately survived.

Today Paul is cancer free. Our family now helps other families who are journeying through the horrors of traumatic brain injury and childhood cancer, raising awareness, hope, and funds for those who are facing major challenges in their lives. My son is a positive force, just like Louise is—he's also helping change the lives of others for the better. Through our hardships, my family has learned a constructive way of thinking: we never take a moment or another person for granted; we live each day with joy, thanksgiving, and hope.

We are sincerely grateful to you, Louise!

⚡ ⚡ ⚡

Doing the Work with Louise

You cannot force your children to be who you want them to be. You cannot make your spouse, parents, siblings, or anyone else change—no matter how well intentioned your actions are. The only person you can change is yourself. Yet when just one person in a home begins to work on loving him- or herself, harmony spreads throughout the family.

If something about your family is causing you unhappiness, your focus may be misdirected. Try directing your attention *inward.* Let go of the beliefs that no longer serve you, those that are keeping you from experiencing self-love. Be an example to your children, your family, and those around you.

These exercises will help work out any issues you have regarding your family. Write your answers on a separate piece of paper or in your journal.

Feelings about Your Family

Think of three events in your life where you feel your family mistreated or abused you. Did someone betray your trust or abandon you when you were in great need? In each case, describe what happened and write down the thoughts you had right before each event occurred.

Now think of three times in your life when you were *helped* by your family. Perhaps someone helped you through a period of grief or loaned you money when you had financial troubles. Explain what happened, and write down the thoughts you had beforehand.

Do you notice a pattern in your thinking?

Rewriting the Past

Think back on your childhood for a moment. Complete the following statements openly and honestly.

1. *My mother always made me . . .*
2. *What I really wanted her to say was . . .*
3. *What my mother really didn't know was . . .*
4. *My father told me I shouldn't . . .*
5. *If my father only knew . . .*
6. *I wish I could have told my father . . .*

Appreciation and Forgiveness

Who in your family have you neglected to acknowledge or appreciate? Take a moment to visualize these people. Imagine looking each person in the eye and saying: *"I thank you and bless you with love for being there for me when I needed you. May your life be filled with joy."*

Are there people you need to forgive? Take a moment to visualize them, too. Look at them in the eye and say: *"I forgive you for not acting the way I wanted you to. I forgive you and set you free."*

Letting Go

Now think of someone in your family you have unresolved issues with. Are you holding on to old anger, grief, or resentment? Write this person a letter. List all your grievances and explain how you feel. Really express yourself, and don't hold back.

After you finish your letter, read it once, fold it, and on the outside, write: *"What I really want is your love and approval."* Then burn the letter and release it.

Self-Worth and Family

Let's examine the issue of self-worth with respect to your family. Answer the following questions as best you can. After each one, say one or more of the positive affirmations that follow to counteract the negative belief.

1. Do you feel worthy of having strong family ties and loving relationships?

2. What do you fear most about getting close to your family?

3. What are you "getting" from this belief?

4. What do you fear will happen if you let go of this belief?

Affirmations

I contribute to a united, loving, and peaceful family life. All is well.

I accept my parents, and they, in turn, accept and love me.

I am a positive example for my own children. We communicate and love freely.

All my relationships are harmonious.

I am open and receptive to all points of view.

Everybody in my family is doing the best they can, including me.

I am willing to forgive the past.

It is safe for me to go beyond my parents' limitations.

As I release all criticism, judgmental people leave my life.

It is safe for me to grow up. I now handle my own life with joy and ease.

I have wonderful, loving, warm, open communication with every member of my family.

I see the best in everyone, and they respond in kind.

My family is loving and supportive.

I send comforting thoughts to everyone and know that these thoughts are returning to me.

I radiate acceptance, and I am deeply loved by others.

I forgive my parents. I know they did the best job they could do.

*I am honest with my family. The more honest I am, the more
   I am loved.*

It is empowering to forgive and let go.

*There is no right or wrong. I move beyond any feelings of
   judgment.*

It is safe for me to be open with myself and my family.

Treatment for Children and Family Issues

*I claim for myself a joyous, loving family. I bless each member of my
family with love. We are all doing the best we can at any given moment.
I choose to open my heart to love, compassion, and understanding to
flush out all memories of past pain. I only allow supportive, nurturing
people in my world. My life is filled with love and joy. This is the truth
of my being, and I accept it as so. All is well in my world.*

Chapter Seven

Learning
to Love

It is a wonderful thing to experience romantic love. However, the most important love we can attain is <u>self</u>-love. Truly loving ourselves means having a deep appreciation for who we are, including what we see as our "faults." It's sad, but many of us refuse to love ourselves until we reach some silly, self-imposed goal such as losing weight or making a lot of money. These goals are only a distraction, masking the true lack in our lives. Ultimately, we cannot sustain healthy relationships with other people if we do not have healthy, loving relationships with ourselves.

I hope that after reading the following stories, you'll begin to love <u>yourself</u> just a little bit more.

The Power of Love
by Stacey, executive assistant/contracts
administrator, California

"You have to love yourself before anyone else will love you." I cringed every time I heard that saying because at a very young age, I learned that I wasn't lovable at all.

My father left my mother when I was four years old; that same year, she tried to commit suicide. My brother, sister, and I were sent to live with our grandparents while our mother recovered in a mental institution. We were sent back to live with her after about a year, but she still wasn't stable enough to take care of her kids. She started drinking and doing drugs—and like most kids who are raised by addicts, we were neglected, and exposed to situations children should never have to endure.

I thought that when I started school I'd be safe for a few hours a day. Unfortunately, because I was poor and had red hair and freckles, I was teased and treated like I was deformed. On Valentine's Day, all of the children in my class exchanged cards, and everyone got valentines but me. I'd lie in bed every night and ask God to make me beautiful so that I could finally be loved.

I did develop into an attractive woman, so then, instead of being teased, I was being told that I was pretty on a regular basis . . . but it didn't matter because I still felt ugly on the inside. Thanks to my low self-esteem, I made some decisions that a lot of people who don't love themselves make. I drank a little more than I should have, chose men who weren't good for me, and passed up some great opportunities.

One day a friend gave me a copy of *You Can Heal Your Life*, telling me that she thought it would help me. After reading it, I started to say affirmations to counteract my negative thoughts and my residual fear. This wasn't easy for me because I'd lived with fear all my life—I was either afraid of losing what I had or not getting what I wanted. But I kept doing the affirmations.

Fast-forward about ten years. While searching for a job, I affirmed: *I have a job that I love, and I am financially secure* . . . over and over to myself. I'd never searched for a job online, but I was led to do so now. I ultimately interviewed for a position that turned out to be the perfect fit for me: executive assistant to the president of Hay House, Inc., which was founded by Louise Hay.

I've been working at Hay House for almost eight years now and it has truly been a blessing. I have a job that I absolutely love, and I am financially secure. I recently bought a house and am even planting a Louise Hay rose in my garden. I'm not that little girl who didn't get a single valentine anymore—I have wonderful friends, and I'm healthy and happy.

I am so grateful for everything Louise has taught me. I can honestly say "I love myself" now . . . and I mean it!

⚡ ⚡ ⚡

Planting the Seeds
by Jennifer, high-school special-education teacher, Wisconsin

Miracles are described as events that appear to be contrary to the laws of nature and are considered to be acts of God. I would indeed say that the changes in my life are nothing short of miraculous, thanks to Louise Hay!

Before I knew about Louise, my relationship with God had deteriorated. I was battling brutal depression, severe mood swings, and relentless migraine headaches. I had struggled with feelings of abandonment since childhood; consequently, I suffered through many years of guilt, self-doubt, fear, worry, self-esteem issues, and lack of love and trust for myself and others.

While searching for some relief, I came across *You Can Heal Your Life,* which reminded me that no one would be able to love me until I could love myself. Louise instructed me how to see, and then love, myself as God does. Her wisdom-filled words showed me how to forgive my parents and to look at them in a new way. As I learned how to be a survivor rather than a victim, years of sadness melted away.

Louise taught me how to be strong by loving myself, and I learned just how powerful this can be. So this is the miracle that I've been blessed with: I love myself! It's not rhetoric or embellishment—it's true! And Louise's gifts keep on giving: As I work with my special-education students, not a day goes by without my passing on her words and wisdom in one way or another. In fact, I ask my students to keep journals full of Louise's powerful affirmations and phrases, which is very empowering. I've seen kids come into my classroom with a dark outlook on life at the beginning of the school year, and then by midyear, they've acknowledged the power of positive thinking. The seeds have been planted!

Louise, you absolutely saved my life. Because of you, depression and insecurity no longer rule my days, and I'm able to be the beautiful person I've always dreamed of. I'm able to have a loving relationship with myself, with God, and with my friends and family members (including my mother, whom I hated for years). I've embraced your words and become a role model for my loved ones, my co-workers, and my students. I'm able to enjoy life and embrace all the happiness around me—I genuinely believe that I deserve that happiness as well. And I'm able to smile and really mean it. Your book truly helped me heal all of the hurt and dysfunction in my life. I am living proof of what happens when someone takes your words, makes them a reality, and comes to genuinely love herself!

✗ ✗ ✗

Transformative Magic
by Dijana, general manager of a
publishing company, Australia

As an astrologer, I'd long been on a journey of self-discovery. When my 15-year marriage hit a critical point, I faced a serious choice: follow *my* truth or his. It was the call that I'd known was coming, but I'd been denying it thus far.

It became clear that the relationship needed to end, and although I thought that my husband and I had "evolved" enough to do so graciously, I was wrong. I found myself walking an emotional minefield, and life threw some serious trials my way. It was time to put all I'd learned over the years into practice. I turned to my copy of *You Can Heal Your Life* in order to change my thoughts and use the power of affirmations.

Along with astrology, I was fascinated by pagan ritual, which honors the earth's energies and feminine principles. I began to augment my affirmations by using planetary energies and ritual to harness anything I wanted to rid myself of—and I was amazed by the results.

On my 41st birthday I conducted a focused ritual, and the most amazing career opportunity just "landed" in my lap, as if by Divine grace, soon after. You see, I work in publishing in Australia and love my job. I'd always had a keen interest in the MBS (mind-body-spirit) genre, though, and it wasn't an area my company dealt with yet.

Then one fateful day, my boss called me into his office and asked me if I'd like to work directly with Hay House and manage the sales of their products in Australia. Knowing that I'd be helping sell the books of the woman who had just profoundly helped *me* caused me to burst into tears. Soon I met the Hay House team in Australia, and it was instantly a marriage made in publishing heaven. A year later, working with Hay House has been my career highlight—topped by the opportunity to have a lovely dinner with Louise herself.

Could it get any better than this? Apparently, it could. Eighteen months after the end of my marriage, I'd progressed to thinking about another relationship. With clear intent, I decided to attract the love I'd always desired, knowing that I now possessed the tools to do so. I was happy, and sharing this joy was my intent.

During a Libran full moon, I used Louise's love affirmations and focused all of my energy into clearly defining what I wanted. I put it out there to the universe to bring me a new love, and I fully trusted in the process. Two weeks later, he arrived.

This man was different, not my usual "type," but I recognized him instantly. The rest is history—he's become the greatest of all loves. He is all I could ever dream of and more, and I honestly feel so blessed and grateful every day.

Thank you, Louise, for providing the tools for true love and complete transformative magic. I am eternally grateful.

A Whole New Way of Living
by Candice, executive assistant, Michigan

In 1993, at the age of 23, I was given *You Can Heal Your Life* by two different people while I was working as an escort in New York City. One of them insisted that I look in the mirror and tell myself, "I love you." It was probably the hardest thing I have ever done.

I was molested as a child by five different men, got pregnant the night before my 15th birthday, and had an abortion. Although I was gifted with intelligence and creativity, I never believed in myself until I began doing the affirmations I found in *You Can Heal Your Life*. That book opened up a whole new way of living for me, and my thoughts began to mirror those in its pages.

I was able to turn my life around, but I might not have been able to do so had I not learned how to love myself and treasure the talents and uniqueness that I possess. Louise gave me the greatest tools necessary for a fulfilling life, and I continue to share her work with other women. I can't thank her enough.

☘ ☘ ☘

Pure, Unconditional Love
by Lareena, accountant, California

My mother abandoned my father, my brother, and me when I was three. The images I have of her are vivid but painful. She loved entertaining multiple men—I remember sitting in a corner pretending to have a conversation with my doll, blocking out noises a young child shouldn't hear.

My dad, my one-year-old brother, and I shared a single bedroom in my grandmother's home. My father also entertained multiple women in the same room we shared, thinking I was peacefully asleep. Dad eventually remarried a psychotic woman, who physically and mentally tortured me and my brother for nine years. My father turned a blind eye; he may have been physically present in my life, but he was emotionally absent for most of it.

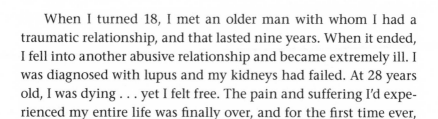

When I turned 18, I met an older man with whom I had a traumatic relationship, and that lasted nine years. When it ended, I fell into another abusive relationship and became extremely ill. I was diagnosed with lupus and my kidneys had failed. At 28 years old, I was dying . . . yet I felt free. The pain and suffering I'd experienced my entire life was finally over, and for the first time ever, I experienced a sense of peace.

Lying in my hospital bed, I knew I was going to die, so I called all of my loved ones into the room and said my good-byes. I said a prayer thanking God for this experience, and then I told Him that I was tired and ready to go Home. I felt myself slipping away, and then I saw the most beautiful white light you can imagine. To my surprise, I woke up in the emergency room, and my pain was completely gone.

I underwent chemo and dialysis four hours a day, four times a week. I was taking 17 different medications, walked with a cane, and was pretty much in bed most of the time. During this period, my auntie gave me a book called *You Can Heal Your Life,* by Louise L. Hay. The main affirmations I used were these: *I speak up for myself freely and easily. I claim my own power. I love and approve of myself. I am free and safe.*

My daily activities included praying, meditating, and visualizing; as well as mirror work, which was extremely difficult. It was very hard to look into my eyes where so much pain was hidden. At one point, I forcefully said out loud, "Lareena, I love you so much. Lareena, I love you just the way you are." The tears poured down uncontrollably—I realized that I was finally receiving pure, unconditional love.

After a while I began to feel things shift deep inside me. I saw myself smiling and laughing, and I felt lighter and brighter. It took six months to fully recover, but the chemo and dialysis treatments have ended. I've regained my kidney function completely, and the lupus has been inactive for the past two years. At 31 years of age, I am perfectly healthy and whole, and all is well in my world!

✐ ✐ ✐

The Priceless Present
by Marina, translator, Russia

I had an inferiority complex for as long as I could remember, thinking that I was "less than" others. But why? I really wanted to know the truth. When I was 13, I discovered Louise Hay's book *You Can Heal Your Life*. At first I didn't understand very much from it, but my inner feelings told me, *This is the right way.* Step by step I began to heal my soul; real changes occurred when I decided to change my thoughts about myself.

During a month-and-a-half period, I repeated affirmations about loving myself more than 400 times a day. And it worked! You may not think that this is a "Wow" story, but when you live with constant pain in your heart that doesn't let you enjoy your life, to feel love in your heart—especially for yourself—is a real wonder. To love yourself is to experience a miracle every day.

My healing process started 15 years ago and hasn't stopped. My life has completely changed, and this was a priceless present Louise gave me. I thank her very much indeed!

᙮ ᙮ ᙮

A Fateful Encounter
by Julie, nurse, Alaska

After going through a few stressful weeks, I knew I had to find the time to browse the New Age section of a bookstore and decompress. One day I decided to do just that before meeting a friend for lunch.

As I was looking through some titles, a man approached me and said, "If you ever get the chance to read a good book, you might like to try this one," pointing to Louise Hay's *You Can Heal Your Life*. My jaw dropped. For the past 25 years, whenever anyone asked me what my favorite book was, I'd answer, *"You Can Heal Your Life."*

As I stood there, my first thought was: *This is an angel encounter, but he isn't what I would have thought an angel would look like.* I went on to tell the man about my love for Louise Hay and this book in particular. After chatting for a few more minutes, we parted ways. But then a clairaudient message came to me, saying: "Don't let him go." With that, I ran after this man and explained how I knew this meeting wasn't by chance. He agreed, telling me that he'd actually gone to the bookstore across town to buy Louise's book for an ailing friend. They were sold out but said that they could order it for him—yet he just *knew* he had to go across town in midday traffic to get a copy of it right away.

That was more than two years ago, and we've been together ever since. We're now engaged to be married, and I tell our story to whoever will listen. Thank you, Louise, and my beloved angels!

✗ ✗ ✗

Loving Myself Was the Answer
by Cynthia, executive assistant, Florida

Nine years ago I came to the United States on vacation and decided to stay. All of my family is in Peru, so the first two years here were very difficult. Then in 2005, I began to experience panic attacks—I had them every day for four months and was just miserable. I traveled to Los Angeles for business and went to a spa, where I found some of Louise Hay's CDs, along with her book *The Power Is Within You.* That title really got my attention.

After I listened to the CDs and read the book, I began to use affirmations a great deal; in particular, I'd repeat *I love myself* over and over again. It wasn't long before I started to see a transformation in my life. By replacing the negative thoughts in my mind with new, positive ones, I realized that I was changing the way I was thinking and seeing life differently.

I was so grateful that I e-mailed Louise, and her assistant responded with a beautiful message full of hope and support. After that I went to a bookstore and bought *You Can Heal Your Life* in

Spanish, along with the *Stress-Free* CD in English (I use this every time I fly, as it relaxes me and puts me to sleep . . . it's amazing how this CD works). I have gone on to enjoy four years without panic attacks.

Louise's books and CDs have helped me realize that learning to truly love myself has been the key to a wonderful life. One of my wishes is to meet Louise in person. I think that she's a wonderful woman who has devoted her life to helping other people such as myself, and I thank her so much.

⚹ ⚹ ⚹

Training My Brain
by Melanie, program coordinator, Canada

Being a logical person in most aspects of my life, I was having a difficult time coping with all the emotions I was having after I left my husband of ten years. Dealing with the sole responsibility for my three children, my career, and my home was overwhelming— I had no idea where to turn or even what it was that I was feeling.

A colleague who'd seen through the act I was putting on recommended *You Can Heal Your Life* to me. It was the first book of Louise Hay's I'd ever read, but certainly not the last. Through her books and various tools, Louise has taught me to train my brain to think positively. I realized that I hadn't really loved myself before . . . and now I do.

Changing my life has been a process, and it has required the use of many different virtues such as patience and determination. Even so, utilizing my intuition as well as logic has been rewarding. My life has flourished due to the change in my thought patterns: I've lost 25 pounds; I no longer suffer from acne; and I appreciate myself and my surroundings without effort, seeing the beauty in things through eyes of love. My new discovery of independence, fun, and love—as well as the commitment to the lifelong process of happiness—is felt by my friends and family. I express my gratitude every day for picking up Louise's book and, indeed, healing my life.

⚹ ⚹ ⚹

The Most Important Miracle of All

by Martin, insurance salesman, Argentina

I am a 30-year-old man who lives in Argentina. *You Can Heal Your Life* came into my life when I was only 15—since then, my life has changed completely.

Waking up to life so young was the best and most important thing that Louise could have done for me. Living in Argentina is not that easy, with our economic woes and terrible poverty. I knew that my life had to be bigger than that, so I vowed to change my mind and my thoughts. I started by affirming: *I am not a statistic* many times a day.

Even though everyone told me, "It's not easy to get a good job here," I knew that I could get a *fantastic* one . . . and I did. I also started to take care of my body by becoming a vegetarian and running every day (at first I couldn't even run a block, and now I participate in marathons several times a year). I began to travel around the world, and I met amazing people who opened my mind to new ideas.

But the miracle that Louise has brought into my life is the incredible love that I feel for myself and others—it is priceless. Louise gave me a whole new existence, and I'll be eternally grateful to her every single day of my life.

We tend to think that miracles are only related to overcoming an illness or other big issues. Yet Louise teaches that miracles are all around us, in every breath, in every smile, in every rose and sunset.

Thank you, Louise, for being my inspiration and introducing us all to the most important miracle of all: the love of ourselves. You are the best!

Bitterness and Pain Lead to Love and Peace
by Margaret, jewelry designer, Maryland

In 1990 I came home to a note from my husband of 15 years saying that he'd left me. I was very upset and confused, feeling that the life I'd lived for a decade and a half had all been a lie. I worked and carried on as I had to, but inside I was extremely bitter, untrusting, and generally hateful toward the world.

One day in 1995, I hit rock bottom when I met someone who was just like me—it was like the Ghost of the Future had visited to show me what I'd end up like if I continued on this path. Having been surrounded all my life by atheists, I had been brainwashed in that direction and had never been a very spiritual person. But that night I got down on my knees and prayed to be shown how to change.

I was first led to Louise Hay's book *You Can Heal Your Life.* I devoured those pages and typed up all of the affirmations and exercises to say out loud. The hardest thing for me to do was to say "I love you, Margaret" in the mirror—that took two weeks.

The spirituality that Louise spoke of opened up a whole new world for me. I had my biggest and most remarkable spiritual awakening after reading *You Can Heal Your Life;* once I got it, there was no turning back. I kept moving forward, learning to release all the hatred, distrust, and aloneness I felt. I was very concerned about my future, so I worked on my feelings of low self-esteem. Then I endeavored to bring some financial abundance into my life, an area that had been challenging up to that point.

The years of work I spent on myself thanks to Louise's book changed my whole life; I'm especially thankful that she taught me to release my bitterness to allow in the good that was waiting for me. I ended up meeting my real soul mate and now enjoy a wonderful, trusting, spiritual relationship and marriage. The best thing my new husband has taught me is unconditional love (the icing on the cake is that he is very wealthy and has given me the financial security I was looking for).

I could have been plodding along, making the same mistakes over and over again—but Louise's book helped me see that there was a better way. She opened my heart to love and made me realize my connection with my spirit. I carry that spirituality with me to this day, and my consciousness has brought me so much peace.

∦ ∦ ∦

Loving Myself Again
by Leah, certified professional coach, Canada

I discovered the work of Louise Hay at a time in my life when I was in the midst of a particularly challenging period, which many refer to as "the quarter-life crisis." I'd been working overseas for more than a year and a half, and I was unsure of my future plans. I wondered when to come home, *if* I should come home, and ultimately where I belonged. I felt isolated and lonely—homesick for family, friends, and familiarity—yet addicted to the thought of yet another country to visit.

Struggling with the stress of what felt like massive decisions in front of me, I started abusing alcohol and food to escape the reality I'd created. I then began to gain weight, making it even more difficult to even consider coming home. I'm ashamed to say that during my lowest period, I turned to drugs in a country where the penalty is severe at best.

One day, on a rare trip to a bookstore to find some English reading materials, I discovered *You Can Heal Your Life*. I was blown away by the concepts and affirmations presented within the pages and began to wonder what it would be like to love myself again.

I started to do some mirror work, telling myself over and over: "I love you, Leah. I really, really love you." Then I just kept on going, using affirmations each and every day.

Slowly, I began to see some amazing changes: I started to value myself, giving myself permission to pursue holidays and trips all over Asia and finally making the decision to go home. New friends appeared in my life, and I met a wonderful coach who helped me lose more than 40 pounds through walking and nutrition. The process was easier and more gentle than I ever could have imagined!

When I eventually returned home to Canada, I believe it was no coincidence that one week after arriving, I met the man who is now my fiancé. I'd attracted the "right kind of man" because, through my development, I'd become the "right kind of woman," one who loves herself.

Louise inspired me to discover my true self as I began the on-going process of self-awareness. Her work has inspired, motivated, and even shaped my career—now I am a certified professional coach with a successful practice, helping other young professionals create purpose and meaning in their lives.

Louise, you've had a tremendous impact on my life. Thank you for being a source of inspiration and healing for so many of us around the globe.

꙰ ꙰ ꙰

Time to Make a Change
by Gloribell, graduate student,
aspiring actress, and mom, New Jersey

You Can Heal You Life changed everything for me. In 2003 I was going through one of the darkest and stormiest times of my life. My six-year marriage was a complete train wreck. My world was closing in fast, and I was convinced that everyone would be better off without me. I felt the tremors and aftershocks of unrelenting pain and sorrow inside of me.

Feeling hopeless and suicidal, I went to the library to find some refuge and peace. I remember seeing a brightly colored book that called out to me. I picked it up and read the title—*You Can Heal Your Life*—out loud. I found myself intrigued by the idea that I could change my thinking and make deliberate choices to be happy. Having always been a very studious and curious person, I decided that I needed to take this book home with me to investigate these ideas.

I read it, reread it, and then read it again. I did not sleep that night, because I had the earth-shattering realization that neither my husband nor I had ever learned how to have a healthy relationship. We both came from abusive homes, so our current state of marital discord and extreme dysfunction was the only thing we were able to create, given our childhood training.

I knew it was time to make a change. I took Louise's advice and found a psychotherapist to help me deal with forgiving my parents, setting boundaries, and redefining myself as a person. At first I did all of this to save my marriage, but as I delved deeper and deeper into the process of self-discovery, I realized that what I really wanted to do was save myself.

I went back to school, gained confidence in myself, and made it my mission to enjoy life. I became healthier, and as a result, my husband improved his own health. There was no formal conversation where we decided, "Okay, let's be healthy and try to work on the marriage"—it just happened on its own. In other words, when I stopped trying to *save* the marriage, the marriage ended up saving itself.

Louise's profound statement, "All is well," was what kept me going. Since she said it with such power and sincerity, I really believed her whenever I got scared. I felt as if she were talking directly to me: "All is well, Gloribell!"

Today I am with my husband because I want to be, not because I have to. I truly love this man, but more important, I truly love *myself.* Our turbulent past and our present-day triumph is really proof of what Louise has said for so many years: "The point of power is always in the present moment."

🖋 🖋 🖋

The Salve for All Wounds
by Renna, writer and model, Finland

I was born in Estonia in 1961, and at that time, my country was part of the Soviet Union. As you might imagine, life was challenging in many ways.

I was a very quiet and introverted girl who had a difficult relationship with my cold and critical mother. Although I discovered meditation as an adult and gave up a decade-long smoking habit, I'd lost some teeth as a young lady and felt very self-conscious. I found myself in a deep depression for a long time.

In the '90s, Louise Hay's books were translated into Estonian. One of them said something to the effect that however dark it is in your mind right now, it's only temporary—the sun still exists and will be shown to you in time. Another thing Louise imparted was that it was never too late to try to heal your relationships. These two thoughts brought me such relief and even gave me spiritual wings. It was as if Louise were the sun herself, shining down through the black clouds of my country and my mind.

I read as much of Louise's works as I could and practiced what she preached. I came to understand that love was the salve for all of my wounds, and I used it to heal the relationship with my mother. I also learned to look at myself with loving eyes and embrace what I saw. I left my dark depression behind and moved into a life of possibility and joy. I'm so thankful for Louise!

❧ ❧ ❧

The Journey to Love
by Misti Marie, educational assistant, Hawaii

My journey began at the age of 16 when I fell in love. I had my son when I was 17 and my daughter when I was 23. Unfortunately, three years into this relationship, I discovered that the "love of my life" was hooked on drugs. (I'd already been dealing with his alcoholism.)

The experiences that resulted from my boyfriend's addictions had a profoundly negative impact—emotionally, mentally, and physically. This unhappiness went on to manifest itself in my life as migraines and anxiety. There was an absence of authenticity, integrity, respect, and commitment in our relationship. There was also a lack of love. Yet I *believed* I was in love, often living in a fantasy world in which I could inspire and motivate my boyfriend to overhaul his life and allow us to keep our beautiful family together. Changing him was my number one priority. And when I wasn't focusing on him, I was being a mother, working on my B.A. in psychology, and being a preschool teacher—all of these roles served as distractions.

There were times when I just went with the flow of things, pretending that I didn't see the destruction of our lives in the hopes that maybe it would all just stop. Then our kids got older, and they started to express their fears, concerns, and feelings in relation to the dysfunction. I knew that a change needed to be made, but I didn't know where I was going to find the strength.

Well, I found that strength the moment my amazing mom gave me *The Power Is Within You,* by Louise Hay. As soon as I began reading this book, I knew that Louise was speaking directly to me. She is an angel who touches your soul, heals your heart, and lifts your spirits. These words she wrote really struck me: "Every day declare for yourself what you want in life. Declare it as though you have it!" At that moment, I realized that I needed to focus on changing *myself,* not my boyfriend.

I immersed myself in self-help products. *You Can Heal Your Life* became my bible, and I'd listen to the *I Can Do It* CD at night. Louise gave me the tools, inspiration, and motivation I needed to take back my power and commit to happiness—what a beautiful concept! I learned that we all actually have choices, and the only moment we have is here and now. Loving ourselves unconditionally and learning to practice the power of forgiveness are essential keys to life.

On our tenth anniversary, I ended the relationship. My kids and I are blessed; and my life is now filled with an abundance of peace, joy, and deep love. I believe this to be true, and so it is! I stand in gratitude for Louise because she has given me the gift of love, forgiveness, and transformation!

❧ ❧ ❧

What One Good Hug Can Do

by Marcela, physician, Spain

I've long wanted to write Louise Hay a note to say thank you for teaching me the most important lesson I've had to learn in this journey. Well, today is that day!

A loving friend gave me her personal copy of *You Can Heal Your Life* as a present during a difficult time in my life. I took a quick glance at the cover with its rainbow heart and thought, *Oh my God, you've got to be kidding me!* To say that Louise wasn't my cup of tea would be an understatement.

But I've discovered that it really is true: "The teacher only appears when the student is ready." Despite my resistance, Louise started appearing in my life again and again and again—until one day I was ready to hear her message.

Despite the outward success and praise I'd enjoyed in life, I now discovered that I didn't love myself. That pill was hard to swallow. So, since I'd been educated as a scientist, I decided to give myself one opportunity to put Louise's ideas to the test. I took a 30-day challenge to say "I love you" in the mirror every day, but I didn't think the experiment was working—I'd usually merely see a stranger on the other side of the mirror, looking at me with indifference. Irritated and feeling worse than I had before I started the challenge, I discarded Louise's message.

Then something happened. I had just moved to a new city and had been having a particularly bad week when my neighbor, whom I'd met less than two months before, gave me a hug. I was stunned, realizing that this was the first physical contact I'd had with anyone in two months. I suddenly saw how deprived I was of love—one hug in two months is only six hugs a year!

I decided to make a small modification to Louise's exercises and try again. This time I actually started hugging myself! First I did four hugs a day, which was very uncomfortable. Nevertheless, I persisted, building up to 8 hugs, then 12, and so on, as if I were weight training. With the hugs came "I love you" and other kind words, along with encouragement and affection for myself.

Hugging myself and saying "I love you" is something very powerful in my life. I just hold myself, like a loving parent cradling a precious child, and I feel safe. Most important, I feel loved. I still have bad days, but now when I have them, I simply remind myself that this is one of those times when I need to love myself more instead of going into a spiral of depression.

I have scheduled hugs into my personal agenda every day and always keep the appointment, knowing that I'm meeting with the most important person in my life. And here's another great thing: when I'm hugging myself at work, most people just think I'm shivering, so I don't even have to give an explanation!

God bless you, Louise.

Doing the Work with Louise

Imagine the perfect relationship, the feeling of being completely head over heels in love. This is what loving yourself is like, minus the burden of having to depend on the actions of another person for fulfillment. Your relationship with yourself is the steadiest, most constant relationship you will ever have—so make it your *best* relationship! You are absolutely worthy of love. It isn't necessary to prove anything or convince anyone of this. Once you recognize yourself as deserving of love, other people will naturally treat you with love, too.

You will be able to further explore your beliefs about love by completing the following exercises. Write your answers on a separate piece of paper or in your journal.

Your Critical Self

Criticism breaks down the inner spirit but never changes a thing. Praise builds up the spirit and can bring about positive change. Write down two ways in which you criticize yourself in the area of love and intimacy. Perhaps you're not able to tell people how you feel or what you need. Maybe you have a fear of commitment, or you tend to attract partners who hurt you.

After each of your perceived faults, think of something you can praise yourself for in this area.

I Love Myself

At the top of your piece of paper or your journal, write: *I love myself; therefore* . . .

Finish this sentence in as many ways as you can. Read it over daily, and add to it as you think of new things. If you can work with a partner, do so. Hold hands and alternate saying, "I love myself; therefore . . ." The greatest benefit of doing this exercise is that it is almost impossible to belittle yourself when you say that you love yourself.

Your Feelings about Love and Relationships

Now answer the following questions as best you can:

1. What did you learn about love as a child?

2. Is your partner/spouse like one of your parents? How?

3. Think about your last two intimate relationships. What were the major issues between you?

4. Do these issues remind you of your relationship with one or both of your parents? How?

5. What or whom would you have to forgive in order to change this pattern?

6. From your new understanding, what would you like your relationship to be like?

Mirror Work

When it comes to loving ourselves, mirror work is extremely effective. When we look in the mirror today, most of us will say something negative to ourselves. We either criticize our looks or berate ourselves for something. It is time to change this habit.

Go to the mirror, look into your eyes, and say the following: *"I love you,* [insert your name]. *I really, really love you."*

Write down what kinds of feelings this brings up in you.

Do this exercise every morning. You will find that it becomes easier and easier to do, and the love in your life will increase in amazing ways.

Love and Intimacy

Let's examine your beliefs about love. Answer each of the questions below. After each answer, say one or more of the positive affirmations that follow to counteract the old belief.

1. Do you feel worthy of having an intimate relationship?
2. Are you afraid to love yourself or others?
3. What are you "getting" from this belief?
4. What do you fear will happen if you let go of this belief?

Affirmations

I am loving and lovable and loved.

I give myself permission to experience intimate love.

I am worthy of love. I now create a long-lasting, deeply caring relationship.

Love and acceptance are mine. I love myself.

I express love, and I always attract love wherever I go.

I am willing to let love in. It is safe to let love in.

The more I open up to love, the safer I am.

I am gentle and loving with myself, and so is my partner.

It is safe for me to be in love.

No one can mistreat me. I care for, appreciate, and respect myself.

People love me when I am myself.

I am loved and safe wherever I go.

I attract wonderful, loving experiences into my life.

I accept myself completely and take care of my inner child.

I love myself and my sexuality.

I see myself with eyes of love, and I am safe.

My partner reflects the love I have for my own body.

I express my desires with joy and freedom. Love makes me feel free.

I give myself permission to enjoy my body.

Loving myself and others gets easier every day.

Treatment for Love

Deep at the center of my being, there is an infinite well of love, joy, peace, and wisdom. I take a moment now to consciously go to that infinite well of love within me. I feel the love that is there, and I let it grow and expand. I claim love and intimacy in my world. I am worthy of love. I am not my parents, nor their own relationship patterns. I am my own unique self, and I choose to create and keep a long-lasting and loving relationship—one that nurtures and supports us both in every way. This is the truth of my being, and I accept it as so. All is well in my loving world.

Part III

Emotions
and Behavior

Chapter Eight

Achieving
Mental Wellness

When you can accept that you choose every thought and feeling you have, then mental health and well-being also become choices. However, accepting <u>responsibility</u> for your thoughts does not mean accepting <u>blame.</u> It only means taking control of your mind by purposely choosing each new thought as a way to love and respect yourself. You don't need to continue acting in a self-destructive way just because it's what you've always done. Instead of reinforcing your old feelings of negativity and hopelessness, you can redirect that energy toward manifesting a better life for yourself, no matter what affliction or challenge you might be facing.

The people in the following stories share how they have overcome many obstacles, both physical and emotional, in their quest for mental wellness.

Mother Energy
by Madisyn, author and editor, Oregon

My mother handed me a cassette tape and said, "Listen to this. It will make you cry."

It was the early 1990s, and I'd been stuck in the mire of my life for a long time. For the past two years, I had been very sick;

doctors didn't know what to do with me, and *I* didn't know what to do with me either. My world had turned into an antidepressant hamster wheel—after I'd max out on the dosage of one medication, I'd be on to another. To make matters worse, my father had just died suddenly, and we hadn't been on speaking terms prior to his death.

I had heard of Louise Hay, as there was a metaphysical bookstore in my neighborhood that I had always been drawn to. I really liked going to that store because it made me feel good. I didn't tend to buy anything, though, since the number of self-help books and gadgets was a bit overwhelming and I simply didn't know what kind of help I needed.

Finally, on a quiet day, I picked up the tape my mother had given me. I inserted it into my handheld cassette player, put on the headphones, and lay down on the sofa, not really knowing what to expect. Upon hearing Louise's voice, I immediately felt like I was being held by "Mother" energy. It wasn't necessarily her *words,* but more the tone of her voice and the intention behind it that made me feel this way. My own mother was right—I did cry.

Listening to that tape touched something in me I didn't even know had been neglected; it opened the door to my journey of healing on that very day. It almost felt as if I'd been given permission to start healing, and somewhere deep inside, I knew that everything would be okay. I immediately paid a visit to the metaphysical bookstore and purchased many guided meditations, and then I spent an hour each day faithfully listening to them.

Slowly, my world started to open, changes occurred, and I met people who could help me the way I needed to be helped. It was a very long process, and I'm still learning and growing to this day. I look back on those early days and know that I couldn't have done it alone—none of us can. And today I'm paying it forward, having become someone who helps others through my work, as well as being an author of Hay House books.

✧ ✧ ✧

Looking at Life in a Different Way
by Jacky, author and home educator, United Kingdom

I am the 51-year-old mother of a beautiful 10-year-old son. I'd like to share my story.

I was fortunate enough to be breast-fed until I was about eight months of age. Then, because my mother was very tired, she wanted to stop feeding me and asked her doctor for help. He suggested that she put a bitter pill on her breasts, which worked. So at this age and stage in my life, I experienced total rejection. I lost my food source—not to mention love, comfort, and bonding with my mother. In fact, my whole life was shattered by this experience.

When I reached the age of four, I had a large growth on my neck and was hospitalized for several months. Parents weren't allowed to stay with their children in those days, so you can imagine how distressed I was at being left there. On the day I was due to return home, the hospital found another growth in my neck and decided to keep me in for another few weeks for investigation. This was extremely upsetting for a little girl like me.

I went on to suffer from depression for a number of years. I was also an alcoholic in my teens, raped three times, and suffered ill health and tumors throughout adulthood. I had numerous severe head injuries due to accidents that occurred while I was drunk. I lived with a man for 17 years, and we used to fight like cats and dogs. When we finally split up, he killed himself with alcohol and drugs.

I met an amazing man when I was 41, and we went on to have a beautiful baby boy (I actually thought I couldn't have children until this point, so this was especially wonderful). After my son's birth, I again suffered ill health: bouts of pneumonia and bronchitis; fainting spells, which led to severe head injuries; and tumors that were treated with the support of a wonderful homeopath. I also had postnatal depression and couldn't feed my son, which devastated me. In addition, I lost my senses of taste and smell for eight years, had terrible ear infections, and always felt run-down.

Then, at the tender age of 50, I discovered Louise Hay. I undertook her Heal Your Life course, and I invested in her books and

CDs. I learned about the power of affirmations, self-love, and forgiveness to heal—and I haven't looked back since.

This wonderful lady and her philosophies gave me the freedom and excitement to look at life in a different way. Nowadays I am rarely ill, and instead of feeling gloomy and depressed, I look at life's experiences as challenges and learning curves and think of the richness that they bring me.

I thank you and love you so much, Louise!

ᶄ ᶄ ᶄ

Louise's Prescriptions
by Carolin, musical artist, writer,
and entrepreneur, California

The work of Louise Hay—namely, her books *You Can Heal Your Life* and *Heal Your Body*—became part of an overall health regimen I embarked on in the mid-1990s. I had just been diagnosed as bipolar by doctors and was seeking a solution beyond prescribed medication.

Nightly, I'd go over any imbalances I had in my body and apply Louise's "prescription" meditations as the cure. Daily, I'd apply one of her affirmations to combat any down feelings I might encounter while going about my business. Along with establishing an exceptional diet and exercise program, I was not only able to get well without medication, but I haven't even been afflicted by a cold for more than a decade now!

Louise's work has been, and will continue to be, a contributing factor in my ongoing wellness. For this and for life itself, I am grateful.

ᶄ ᶄ ᶄ

New Life Is Born
by April, writer and artist, Georgia

Little black rain cloud. The proverbial "prophet of doom and gloom." Confrontational. Hopeless. This was me before I became aware of Hay House four years ago. For some, life lessons come easy; for others (like me), a war has to be chosen, waged, and won. It's an impossible and incredibly naïve notion to believe that we can conquer our demons with self-loathing, a cardboard sword, and a bad attitude. If anything, the problems become worse, and we sink even deeper into the quicksand of our darker selves.

I'd spent the majority of my life searching for my spiritual sea legs, and it took nearly 20 years of self-inflicted pain and anguish to accept and love myself, leading me to find my place in this world. Diagnosed with bipolar disorder as a young adult, I barged through life without the slightest concern for the wreckage I was leaving in my wake. Chaos swirled around me like parched tumbleweeds in a ghost town, blinding me from seeing my way out of the choking dust. Not until I turned to face my disease and take responsibility for my life did the journey begin.

I began to fumble my way through the darkness toward a pin-hole of light, and in the process, I found seeds of hope that had been sown in the form of prose. Dr. Wayne Dyer challenged me to change my thoughts, inspiring me to realize my ultimate calling —becoming a writer. Deepak Chopra taught me to live my life without limits, allowing me to recognize and humbly accept the power of my intuition. And Doreen Virtue's *Angel Therapy® Oracle Cards* became an integral part of the foundation on which my self-healing was built. Louise Hay's profound influence on my life, however, has not been confined within the pages of a book.

My journey to healing was born out of a traumatic childhood. My teen years were marked by profound angst and depression. My early adult life was riddled with addiction, suicide attempts, and mental illness. It was out of this polluted embryo that my new life was born. It couldn't have happened any other way. Louise helped me see that to heal my body, I had to first heal my mind, quite literally. I had to peel away old layers of myself to find the purity that had been stained by a life of dark influence. The leading force of my remarkable recovery and management of my bipolar disease is a direct result of my unabashed faith—along with the rebirth of my mind, body, and soul.

Louise's vision has helped me find my own. To say "Thank you" would not be enough. So I'll simply repeat the words that she spoke to me through her writing, the words that made me sit up and begin releasing myself from the self-imposed limitations holding me back from my Authentic Self: "If you accept a limiting belief, then it will become the truth for you."

꒰ ꒱ ꒰

Hope
by Malva, fitness instructor, life coach,
and psychologist, Florida

I was born in Montevideo, Uruguay. My mother had the sweetest voice that nurtured my soul and warmed my heart. The last time I saw her, I was only five, because she died of cancer. My world became empty and lonely, and then it became unbearable when my father died from a heart attack. I felt that there was no place in the world for me, and I had no one to turn to. Like many kids in a third-world country, I was homeless, starving for food and love, and simply trying to survive.

When I was a teenager, I managed to get a menial job. One day I found a half-full bottle of Valium and I took all the pills that were left, determined to end my agony. I woke up in the hospital crying because I was still alive, with a little plastic bag with my few belongings in it. I was told that the people I worked for didn't want to be in charge of a teenager with emotional problems and were going to let me go. I felt worse than ever before, thinking that next time, I'd cut my wrists.

And then a nurse brought me the miracle that saved my life: *You Can Heal Your Life,* by Louise Hay. I read it and felt something tingle in my body, my soul, and my heart. For the first time that I could remember, I felt hope.

Louise became the mother I lost as well as my friend, so I got my hands on as many of her products as I could. Not only did I read her books, but I listened to her voice and carried her affirmation cards with me all the time, giving them out whenever the need arose.

Ever since I've been introduced to Louise, so many miracles have come to my life:

— I learned to take care of the lonely, insecure child who was always crying inside me.

— I liberated myself from my negative thinking, guilt, sorrow, and sadness.

— Although I was still just a teenager, I worked hard to help others; when the opportunity arose, I went to college and became a psychologist.

— After discovering that the mind, body, and soul are all one entity, I became a fitness instructor. I talked to people about the way just changing their way of thinking could change their lives.

— I went from extreme poverty to a comfortable position, but my heart and soul were looking for some purpose and meaning, so I chose to give up my financial security for internal freedom and peace. Now I volunteer at hospitals whenever I can. I especially like to spend time with children so that I can give them love and encourage them to keep going. A few months ago, I decided to invest each second of my life in spreading the word that there is hope for everyone.

Thank you, Louise. Today I talk, breathe, eat, sleep, and move with you in my heart. I love you.

❧ ❧ ❧

The Call of My Soul

by Marina, student, Spain

My connection with Louise Hay started in 2002 in a curious way, when I felt very lost and was looking for somebody or something to help me. I still remember the details of how I discovered *You Can Heal Your Life* at the age of 23. I'd gone to stay at a friend's place and said out loud, "Please, I need help!" I looked over at the bookshelf, and there it was! This was just the beginning—later, I found out that miracles are everywhere.

At that point in my life, I was desperate. I'd experienced severe depression for more than a year, and I'd been suffering from anorexia and bulimia since I was a child. I really felt like a mess. I read Louise's entire book over the course of the weekend I spent at my friend's house, and I was in shock for some time. Nobody in my life had ever told me that my thoughts could create anything, so I simultaneously felt angry because I couldn't accept this idea and amazed for all the good that it could bring if I gave it a try.

The next step was to buy the book for myself and start doing Louise's affirmations. The hardest thing for me to do was to say the phrase "I love myself." It's a short statement, but it can be hard for the mind to accept. With time, I realized that if I wanted to overcome my depression and eating disorder, I needed to start loving myself. So I did!

I can assure you that I have never again had the problems that once made my life so miserable. Now when I see that my eating is not going very well or I'm having difficulty with some situation, I remember not to be afraid, that this is just the call of my soul. Louise's affirmations helped me see that there is no need for treating myself with hatred or for punishing myself.

There have been many people in my life who have helped me, and I am very grateful to all of them. But your message, Louise, so clear and direct, was the foundation for my healing. Thank you so much for all the work that you have done and are still doing. You changed my life for the better, and I send you lots of love.

❧ ❧ ❧

Positive Brainwashing

by Janet Rebecca, real-estate agent, Alabama

I first read *You Can Heal Your Life* when I was 18. I'd struggled with suicidal depression for more than two years, on and off, after my father died. I'd also endured a very unhappy childhood filled with religious criticism and rejection—I was shamed for being overweight and told that I had no talents.

I'd been prescribed many different antidepressants, but they never worked. Then I found Louise Hay's book, which gave me power I had no idea I even possessed. The idea that I had choice and responsibility concerning all I believed broke me wide open.

I began my own positive brainwashing to rid myself of the negative beliefs I'd been brought up with. I realized first that God is love—*unconditional* love that I cannot comprehend—and second that I am God's child before I am my parents' child. I was overwhelmed by all the possibilities these realizations brought with them: freedom, peace, and love without limits; beauty and prosperity, both inside and out; inexhaustible strength; and intelligence from on high. I set out to disprove what I'd been taught my whole life: that I was worthless, useless, dumb, ugly, and fat; and I could never support myself financially.

I was finally able to recognize beauty within myself and became a successful model—I actually got paid for my looks! I then went on to become a real-estate professional at age 21, and proved my inherited intelligence and wisdom from God by becoming a millionaire by the time I was 28. I began to attract people and relationships that added to me (and them) instead of being destructive.

I'm now 34, and as I look back, I see that my journey has definitely taken me to places I never dreamed of. But thanks to Louise, I've learned to never put limits on anything I work on. Of course, I have had my share of struggles and have certainly had my doubts, but I never gave up. After 16 years of study and reflection on myself, I'm ready to go even deeper and willing to see where life will take me next. I believe more than ever in Louise's teachings!

ᛣ ᛣ ᛣ

A Life of Blessings

by Judie, spiritual being, Hawaii

Here's what I believed before I discovered Louise Hay:

- I was a mistake.

- My sister and I fought too much.

- My mother took her own life because: (a) I was born, and (b) my sister and I fought too much.

- My mother didn't love me enough to stick around and raise me.

- Mom was schizophrenic, and since it's hereditary, I should never have children.

- I was never good enough.

- No one liked me.

- I wasn't worthy of my father's approval.

- I would always be abandoned.

- I was a liar.

- I didn't have the right to have boundaries for my body or my personal possessions.

- I could never be trusted.

- I was unlovable.

At age 21, I was diagnosed with *anxiety neurosis* and began my first round of therapy. After a year, I was able to realize that I wasn't responsible for my mother's suicide, and I was able to forgive myself for thinking that I was.

At age 29, I prayed, "Lord, if you want me to spend the rest of my life alone, you'll have to teach me how. But if you want to do it my way, send me someone who is mentally, emotionally, and spiritually healthy!" Then along came Greg, and I never looked back.

Although I've had lots of unconditional love from Greg and our two children, I still felt like a car going down the street with three full tires and one flat—something was missing. Then a friend of mine gave me Louise Hay's book *You Can Heal Your Life,* and the real forgiveness process started. I ultimately came to understand that my parents had done the best they knew how with the tools they'd been given by their own parents.

Louise also helped me realize that I needed to connect with my inner child. I located her wrapped in the fetal position in the linen closet. Taking her by the hand, I brought her out into the light and showed her all the people who loved *me,* and would love *her* as well. I promised her that I was there to protect her and would never let anyone hurt her again.

I am truly blessed that Louise came into my life. Here I am at age 60: I've had 30 wonderful years of marriage; I have two loving, creative kids; I live in Hawaii; and I love my life. I feel incredibly blessed, and I know that the Universe has even more blessings for me.

I want everyone reading this to realize that you too can heal your life with Louise, and all the tools she offers. Don't be afraid— take her hand, and she will guide you through it. And remember to ask your angels for assistance. They want to help you—they just need you to ask.

🖋 🖋 🖋

Getting My Power Back
by Christopher, artist, writer, and
inspirational speaker, Belize

As a little boy, I valued and respected life. I loved the tiny island I was born on; its plants and animals were special to me. I rejected violent games and fighting with my peers. My mother told me that when I was little, I sang upon waking up every morning. I believed the world was beautiful.

Between the ages of three and eight, however, I had several experiences that closed me up emotionally. I don't remember all that occurred, but I do recall being found naked in a cardboard box with two girls twice my age. I vividly remember the punishment I received: I was made to kneel on a steel grate that covered a drain right inside our back door. To ensure my humiliation, I had to kneel naked, facing the open door. It seemed the whole neighborhood came to laugh at me that day, hurling insults at my private parts. The damage to my self-esteem would not show itself until many years later, though.

I buried that shameful memory until I ended up in the hospital at age 24, diagnosed with bipolar disorder. My life turned into a nightmare of hospitalization and drug therapy. Even after I'd been in mental institutions 27 times, I believed that there were alternative choices with respect to my mental health. I had strong faith and was open to trying different methods to achieve wellness—and then my girlfriend introduced me to Louise Hay and her book *You Can Heal Your Life.*

Louise's story touched me deeply, and I could absolutely identify with her early suffering and self-esteem issues. The fact that she could release resentment and forgive all the people in her life gave me the courage to look at the anger I held against my father and so many others, whom I allowed to take my power away. I learned that abuse in childhood happens more from ignorance than anything else. So in my father's mind, his discipline was an attempt to teach me self-respect as a young boy. Louise gave me the courage to accept myself and see God as a loving presence that welcomes me the way I am. I was able to transform my thoughts and heal my mind using the affirmations in her book.

Today I am living proof of the concepts Louise writes about. I am completely healed and drug free, and I live on the beautiful island of Belize doing what I love to do every day. I am a successful artist, writer, and inspirational speaker, serving others with my books and art. Through faith, prayer, hard work, research, and Divine guidance, my angels came to my rescue. Louise Hay is one of those angels.

⚮ ⚮ ⚮

Building My Very Best Life
by Jody Lee, sales representative, California

At the age of 31, I found myself separated from an emotionally abusive man. I had two small children under the age of three, one of whom had serious medical issues and was in and out of the hospital. I was overweight and unemployed, with a mortgage payment, court battles, and a vehicle that soon became inoperable. As depression and feelings of hopelessness set in, I sought counseling for myself and my children. It was while waiting for an appointment that I picked up Louise Hay's book *You Can Heal Your Life* and read a few pages. I couldn't afford to buy my own copy, so the therapist gave it to me.

As I read Louise's book and got in the habit of saying affirmations on a daily basis, I started to feel better. Within a short period of time, I took up running, something I hadn't done since I was 13. My depression lifted, and the desire to be as healthy as I possibly could, both inside and out, grew. I re-enrolled in school and took yoga and other classes of interest that challenged me (something I never would have done before). All the while, I read *You Can Heal Your Life* over and over. It became my bible.

Soon the tired look I'd been carrying around left my face. I lost 25 pounds and felt young again. My grades were higher than they'd ever been, as was my interest in my education. Old friendships were renewed, along with my outlook on life. I also began a healthy relationship with my stepfather after 18 years of ill feelings toward him. I was a completely different person who had lots of love to give and received it well, too. In the past, I'd been so isolated and reserved that I found myself rejecting people because I didn't feel worthy. Now all of that had changed within me.

I felt very empowered. When my son developed behavioral issues, I posted affirmations on his bedroom walls. As I drove him to school, I'd have him look into the mirror on the sun visor and repeat affirmations out loud. Once on the way to a wrestling match, he voiced his feelings of defeat before he even got on the mat. We were still driving when I flipped open the mirror on his visor and started helping him with affirmations. That day he placed second in the tournament. I believe it was then that he realized for the first time just how powerful affirmations can be, and he became willing to continue working with them, even in high school.

Louise, it's now been 20 years since I first picked up *You Can Heal Your Life,* and I want to thank you for bringing me back to life when I was dying inside. I was only 31, yet I felt like I was 91. I want to thank you for providing me with the necessary tools for building my very best life.

⚹ ⚹ ⚹

The Upward Spiral

by Dalon, correctional officer, Texas

For years I'd been battling severe mental illness, and I was almost ready to kill myself because I was in such misery. I decided to give acupuncture a try, telling the practitioner that I was willing to do whatever it took so that I wouldn't have to live like this anymore. He handed me a copy of *You Can Heal Your Life,* and my life turned around.

I had to go through the book several times before I really started to grasp some things; I was having so many bad reactions to all of the medications I was taking, and it was hard for me to figure things out. But I kept at it, and I've been able to create so much more peace and organization in my mind. I went on to pick up Louise's *Love Your Body* cassette tape, and it also made a tremendous impact. The first time I listened to it, I couldn't help but cry, thinking about how I hadn't been loving my body.

I experienced complete acceptance for the very first time during a mirror exercise—I realized that I deserved to be happy and healthy. It's amazing what affirmations, mirror work, love, and time can do. I'm really enjoying being me now, which I don't think I've ever experienced other than when I was a baby. I hold on to my positive affirmations more often than not, and when I do slip back into the old negativity, I don't beat myself up or blame myself. Yes, there are plenty of hurdles and bumps in the road, but I've discovered that while I can always count on myself, I'm never alone.

I'm so proud of myself for sticking with all of this healing work and allowing it to take me on its upward spiral. I'm now working on learning to be gentle with myself and others. This has been a huge challenge in my job as a prison guard.

Recently, an inmate threatened me because I couldn't give him water when he wanted it. When I was able to do so, I came back to his cell to give him the water. He was still very aggressive and refused it. I looked him in the eyes and told him that I forgave him for everything he'd said to me. He just looked down and said thank you. I kept remembering that he was really a brutalized, tormented child. It touched me that by saying three simple words—*I forgive you*—I could put a positive image in the darkened mind of a person who's probably never experienced any kindness in his life.

I love Louise (and Hay House), and one day I would absolutely love to give her a hug for the work she's done. I don't feel empty inside anymore, and I am blessed beyond my fondest dreams. I have my life back, and I feel like I am the luckiest man in the world!

۷ ۷ ۷

The Angel Who Saved My Life
by Natalie, entrepreneur, Utah

Born into a strict and controlling religion, at the age of 18 I'd been betrothed to a polygamist male 15 years older than myself. His first wife and I were like fire and ice; after two years of marriage, suicide seemed the only (and easiest) form of escape. Although my religion had taught me that I'd go to hell if I committed such an act, even that seemed better than this world I'd been subjected to.

My days would begin with tears. By the time I'd get to work, I'd be bouncing off the walls with joy, only to start crying again. Manic depression consumed me, and I often climbed under my desk to hide my sobbing. I hated my life but didn't have the courage to do anything about it, since that would mean challenging my beliefs and walking away from everything I knew.

And then I discovered *You Can Heal Your Life* in the bathroom cupboard at work. I didn't take it because it didn't belong to me, yet I couldn't stop thinking about it. Finally, I borrowed it and read the whole thing in one sitting. It's no exaggeration to say that this book went on to become my bible. From the second I woke up in the morning to the moment I fell asleep, I'd silently repeat my affirmations—if I stopped for just an instant, I'd get an anxiety attack and begin crying all over again.

After only a few weeks, I noticed everything in my life changing. I learned to love myself, and my moods stabilized. I also gained the courage to stand up to authority, including my husband. In six months I was able to take control of my life, and here are a few of the amazing things that happened: Money started to flow to me from all directions so that when the time came for me to take my daughter and leave, I had everything I needed to go. When my car ran out of gas, my tank miraculously filled back up. And I had many experiences where I could command the elements around me and open locked doors.

You Can Heal Your Life has been one of the greatest blessings in my life. To this day I find myself repeating my affirmations and using Louise Hay's wisdom to help me. I've become grateful for the challenges I've been given because they've helped me learn what I needed to become a brighter light here on Earth.

Louise, you are an angel who saved my life. I know with all my heart that God sent your book to me; now, at the age of 26, I have the wisdom and strength to help others. The lessons I learned from your book can never be repaid with any amount of money, but I am paying it forward the best way I can. Thank you, and may God continue to inspire you.

K K K

The Way to True Healing
by Divna, professor of mathematics, Yugoslavia

In 1992 I was 45 years old, married with two kids, and working as a professor of mathematics. Then I got very sick and lost the sight in both eyes. It turns out that I had *neuro-uveitis* and was treated with corticosteroids by ophthalmologists in Belgrade, which is more than 200 miles away from where I live.

Thankfully, doctors were able to restore my sight, but as a side effect of the corticosteroid therapy, my hormonal status became seriously unbalanced. Then in 1997, I had an operation on my thyroid and parathyroid glands to remove a benign tumor. I'm sure I don't have to tell you how awful I felt back then.

At the time of the NATO bombing of Serbia in 1999, I needed to return to the doctors for more treatment, and I was given a hormone that stimulates the adrenal glands. Then I discovered that my husband was having an affair. This broke my heart, and I fell into a state of clinical depression. The doctors thought that all those hormones I'd received contributed to my state, but I was sent to a psychiatric institute in Belgrade anyway.

I met many women there who were depressed just like me, and one of them recommended that I read *You Can Heal Your Life.* As soon as I left the hospital, I bought a copy and read it right away. Louise Hay became my savior! Her book helped me realize that all diseases come from the unwillingness to forgive, which was an absolute revelation for me.

I subsequently bought and read all of Louise's books that had been published in the Serbian language. Louise opened my mind to a totally new perspective and showed me the way to true healing. I went on to read almost everything that had been translated to the Serbian language from several similar authors, such as Susan Jeffers, Shakti Gawain, Deepak Chopra, Jack Canfield, Mark Victor Hansen, and DON Miguel Ruiz.

Little by little, good things started to happen to me. First of all, I became very close to my daughter. She'd also been going through a difficult period of her life at the time, and Louise's book made a great impact on her as well. (She ultimately became a medical doctor—maybe my illness influenced her path?) I understood that the "bad" things that had happened in my life had actually resulted in the highest good, because I learned to love myself. Then I was able to heal myself *and* my life.

I feel pretty good now. I still have sight problems, but the important thing is that the very core of my being—my heart and soul—is healed. God bless you, Louise. I am immensely grateful to you.

✒ ✒ ✒

Doing the Work with Louise

Be patient with yourself as you go through the process of changing your thoughts. Change is gradual; expecting instant results from yourself will only frustrate and discourage you. Allow the process to unfold naturally, and take each step when you're ready for it. Also, remember that it is not necessary to do everything on your own. It is truly an act of self-love to accept help from others when you need it.

You can begin your journey toward mental peace and health by completing the exercises below. Write your answers on another sheet of paper or in your journal.

Dealing with Suppressed Anger

Depression is anger turned inward. It is also anger that you feel you do not have the right to have. For instance, you may feel that it's not okay to be angry at your parent or spouse or employer or best friend. Yet you *are* angry. And you feel stuck. That anger becomes depression. Far too many people today suffer from depression, even chronic depression.

One of the best ways to deal with depression is to give yourself permission to express some of your anger so that you don't have to remain in this state. It can be very helpful to beat your pillows or scream aloud; do be sure that you're *releasing* that anger as you're expressing it.

When you're releasing anger, it's okay to be embarrassed about it, especially if it was against your family rules to get angry. It will be embarrassing the first time you do it, but when you get into it, it can be quite fun and very powerful. God is not going to hate you for being angry.

Once you have released some of this old anger, you will be able to see your situation in a new light and find new solutions. Write down your findings on your piece of paper or in your journal.

Make a List and Forgive

Next put on some soft music—something that will make you feel relaxed and peaceful—and let your mind drift. Go back into the past and think of all the things that you're angry with *yourself* about. Write them down. Write them *all* down. You may discover that you've never forgiven yourself for the humiliation of wetting your pants in the first grade. What a long time to carry *that* burden!

Sometimes it's easier to forgive others than to forgive ourselves. We're often much harder on ourselves and demand perfection. Any mistakes we make are severely punished. It's time to go beyond that old attitude. Mistakes are the way we learn. If we were perfect, there wouldn't be anything to learn. We wouldn't need to be on the planet.

Being "perfect" will not bring you others' love and approval—it will only make you feel "wrong" and not good enough. Lighten up and stop treating yourself that way. It's time to forgive yourself. Let it go. There's no need for shame and guilt in your life. You are free.

Get to Know Your Inner Child

Many of us have an inner child who is lost and lonely and feels so rejected. Perhaps the only contact we've had with our inner child for a long time is to scold it and criticize it. Then we wonder why we're unhappy. We cannot reject a part of us and still be in harmony within.

Part of healing is to gather all the parts of yourself so that you may be whole and complete. Let's do some work so you can connect with these neglected parts of yourself.

1. Look at a photo. Find a photograph of yourself as a child. If you don't have one, ask your parents or other family members to send you one. Study this picture closely. What do you see? It might be joy, pain, sorrow, anger, or fear. Do you love this child? Can you relate to him or her? Write a few words about your inner child.

2. Draw a picture. Now create your own picture of yourself as a child, using crayons, colored pencils, or whatever you prefer. Do be sure to use your nondominant hand (the one you don't write with), however, because it will help open up your more creative side.

3. Describe your creation. What does the picture you created tell you? What colors did you use? What is the child doing?

4. Talk to your inner child. Take a little time now to speak to your inner child. Discover more about him or her. Ask questions, looking into a mirror if you can. Here are some suggestions:

- What do you like?
- What do you dislike?
- What frightens you?
- How do you feel?
- What do you need?
- How can I help you feel safe?
- How can I make you happy?

5. Use visualization. With your eyes closed, picture yourself embracing your inner child. Tell him or her that you are there and will do whatever you can to take care of his or her needs forever.

Have Fun with Your Inner Child

When you're in a state of anxiety or fear that keeps you from functioning, it may be because you've abandoned your inner child. Think of how you could reconnect with him or her now. What could you do together? What could you do that is *just for you?* Write down 15 ways in which you could have fun with your inner child. You might enjoy reading good books, going to the movies, gardening, keeping a journal, or taking a long bubble bath. Really take the time to think about this.

After you've completed your list, try out a few of these "child-like" activities. Find a playground and swing on a swing, draw pictures with crayons, or climb a tree. Go outside and let yourself run. Really run wild and free—turn somersaults, skip along the street—and laugh while you're doing it! Take your inner child with you and have some real fun. So what if someone sees you? Being free is the most important thing!

Try at least one activity from your list each day. You *can* begin to create a happy childhood. Let the healing begin!

Self-Worth and Mental Health

Now let's examine the issue of self-worth with respect to your mental wellness. Answer the following questions. After each one, say one or more of the positive affirmations that follow to counteract the negative belief.

1. Do you feel you deserve mental health?

2. What do you fear most about your health?

3. What are you "getting" from this belief?

4. What do you fear will happen if you let go of this belief?

Affirmations

My mind creates my experiences. I am unlimited in my ability to create good in my life.

I accept all my emotions, but I choose not to wallow in them.

Fear and sadness are merely thoughts, and thoughts can be changed.

My mind is clear and untroubled.

I give myself permission to be at peace and accept the perfection of my life.

I am in control of my emotions and my spiritual growth.

I see my patterns, and I choose to make changes.

I am safe in the Universe, and all life loves and supports me.

I am willing to free myself from the past.

I have the power, strength, and knowledge to handle everything in my life.

It is safe for me to express, and then release, my anger.

I allow life to flow through me. I am at peace.

I am willing to move forward with ease.

I now create new thoughts about myself and my life.

I no longer criticize myself; my mind is at peace.

I love and approve of myself.

I take responsibility for my own life. I am free.

I comfort my inner child, and we are safe.

I deserve to have a wonderful life.

I am safe and secure at all times. Love surrounds me and protects me.

Treatment for Mental Wellness

I claim for myself emotional well-being at all times. I am my best friend, and I enjoy living with myself. Experiences come and go, but I am always here for myself. I choose to think thoughts that are peaceful, joyous, and uplifting. I am my own unique self; and I move through life in a comfortable, safe, and peaceful way. This is the truth of my being, and I accept it as so. All is well in my heart and my mind.

Chapter Nine

Transforming
Old Beliefs

Every day brings with it infinite opportunities for transformation. Yet many of us seem either unable or unwilling to budge from our old habits, even when we're stuck in patterns of pain. Some of us are afraid to let go of what is familiar, no matter how distressful it is. Or, we get so caught up in just getting through each day that we don't even realize there is *any other way.*

We get a chance to change with each new thought we think, because each new thought is a choice. *We can choose a thought that perpetuates negativity, or we can choose a thought based on love. Creating a wonderful new life begins with accepting that we are already wonderful and deserve nothing but good.*

The following stories demonstrate how drastically life can improve once a person moves past his or her old beliefs.

Changing My Destiny
by Irina, holistic counselor, Australia

I was born in Russia in 1970. When I was 18, I got married; when I was 20, my husband, little girl, and I emigrated to Israel. In 1994 I reluctantly agreed to emigrate again, to Australia.

My husband was emotionally and physically abusive, and I became depressed and lonely. After I discovered a melanoma on my right arm, my husband left me for a woman I'd thought was my friend. I became a single mother in a new country—I hardly spoke English, I didn't have a place to live or any money, and I didn't have any relatives or friends. All I had was my six-year-old daughter.

At age 28, I was diagnosed with seven malignant tumors in my lungs and spine. I was told that I had five to eight months to live, and that my chance of survival was 1 in 10,000. I discovered a Russian edition of Louise Hay's book *You Can Heal Your Life,* and it helped me change my destiny. *Why can't I be that 1 in 10,000?* I wondered. I wanted to heal, and Louise taught me how.

The first thing I did was work on forgiving my ex-husband and letting go of all the pain he'd ever caused me. I also nurtured my fragile body (like Louise had done herself) with nutrients, self-love, meditation, prayers, affirmations, and joyful activities with my daughter. Eventually, the tumors vanished, and I went on to find as many of Louise's books as I could.

Inner Wisdom offered me insight into why all of this had happened to me; *Letters to Louise* helped me feel loved; *Heart Thoughts* provided me with daily motivation; and *Empowering Women* inspired me to become a positive and assertive woman with the ability to make her own choices. And this affirmation brought me back to life and created the path to my success: *All is well. Everything is working out for my highest good. Out of this situation, only good will come. I am safe!*

Louise became a true source of inspiration in my life. I learned to trust life, and life began taking care of me. Just a year after first reading *You Can Heal Your Life,* I met and fell in love with a Pakistani Muslim man (even though I'm Jewish!), who became my spiritual partner and best friend. We've been married for nine years now, and despite the doctors' advice, I had another daughter. These same doctors can't explain my miraculous recovery. But I know that when you believe, *anything* is possible!

I'm grateful to cancer because it changed my life for the better, and I'm grateful to Louise, who became my greatest teacher. She taught me how to change my thoughts and beliefs, as well as how to love myself. Today I'm a holistic counselor who helps others turn their own painful experiences into power, and I have an enormous passion for this work. "You can do it," I tell them. "Louise Hay did it, I did it, and so can you."

𝒦 𝒦 𝒦

Internal Freedom
by Adam, artist, California

I am a 30-year-old man who has been surviving in a concrete cage since the age of 16. Behind these cold walls, I've experienced little compassion and healing. The only relief I've felt has come in the form of inmate-made alcohol and the many drugs that circulate throughout a prison system.

One wonderful day nearly three years ago, I was introduced to Louise Hay by my spiritual teacher, whom I was corresponding with. This very compassionate woman shared with me her awe of Louise and explained how she'd changed her own life. My loving friend was very persistent in telling me about Louise's work. Then while I was in "the hole" two years ago, I became inspired by the many life-altering affirmations in *You Can Heal Your Life*. I learned that if I wanted a change, then *I* must do the changing; by doing so, others around me would change how they related to me.

I began to practice affirmations and forgiveness. I was surprised by how repeatedly writing an affirmation brought about the power of transformation. I realized I was worthy of love and healing—and, miraculously, I found internal freedom!

Another profoundly effective tool I'm using these days is the *Love Yourself, Heal Your Life Workbook*. As I've gone through it, Louise has helped me understand myself more by recognizing my character defects and positively transforming them. I'm working on healing my internal wounds, nurturing my mind and heart, and caring for my inner child. Others are astonished by the marked changes I'm now making for the better.

I joyfully receive books from Hay House, which add hope and bright colors to my life. They sure do wonders to enhance my conscious awareness—I have expanded immensely. I've also brought these books to the attention of my clinician here, who approves of them and has made them available to other very needy inmates.

I truly have much better self-esteem and a more positive outlook on life now, and I love to start every day with an affirmation from Louise's book *Everyday Positive Thinking*. Louise has shown me that I have the power to heal myself, and the fact that I am healing more each day is a miracle to me.

Louise, thank you for the immense positive effect you've had on my life, in a place where compassion hardly exists at all.

⚡ ⚡ ⚡

A New Idea and a New Path
by Cheryl, elementary-school teacher, Michigan

Louise Hay seemed to come into my life when I needed her most, just like a little miracle. I guess you could say that I was going through my "quarter-life crisis." To everyone around me, I seemed fine; but deep down inside, I was falling deeper into a hole, and I didn't know how to climb out.

I'd graduated with highest honors from college, married my high-school sweetheart, had a wonderful honeymoon in Mexico, and moved into a lovely new place. All of a sudden these great things were over, though, and I began to feel a lot of anxiety. It seemed that if I could just find a job, most of my problems would go away. Then when I wasn't able to find work right away, I felt like I'd lost my independence. I was now considered a "housewife" at 23, which was not what I wanted. I had to create my own path, but I didn't know how. I felt stuck.

Then in February 2008 I happen to catch an episode of *The Oprah Winfrey Show,* which featured Louise as a guest. Right away I felt as though I was meant to be watching. When Louise spoke, it was like she was talking directly to me. I was intrigued by the title of her book *You Can Heal Your Life.* The fact that we could create our own happiness by changing our thoughts and beliefs was an incredible concept for me! This new idea gave me hope that I could climb out of my hole and begin to love life again.

As soon as I could, I bought a copy of Louise's book. I related to so many things within its pages. Whenever I felt overwhelmed, stressed, sad, or just wanted to continue my healing, I would pick up the book and would instantly feel better. I began to do affirmations daily and eventually memorized my favorite ones so that I had them with me everywhere I went.

Louise's own story in the book was especially inspirational for me. I remembered that when she was diagnosed with cancer, one of the ways she healed herself was through therapy. I felt as though I needed to do more to continue my success, so I began to see a therapist myself. Talking to a professional was just another stepping-stone on my path to healing.

The more I practiced, the more I began to see positive changes in my life. As Louise has said, I was starting to see miracles pop up out of the blue: I soon got a job, my relationship with my husband improved, and my sister and I became close again. My anxiety decreased, and I began to focus on what I really wanted in life. Although I'm still working on myself, I've shared what I've learned from Louise with others—now my family is reading *You Can Heal Your Life* and learning about the power of new beliefs for themselves. I feel so blessed to have found Louise!

ϰ ϰ ϰ

My Best Self

by Eva Marie, professional vocalist, Kentucky

The point of power is always in the present moment. Words like these (and many others) spoken by Louise Hay have helped me change my life, love myself, and continue to grow more into my best self—not to mention connect to the Divine in everything and everyone, each and every day.

In the fall of 2008 my father was diagnosed with terminal lung cancer and was told that he only had a year or two at most to live. This news was truly devastating for my family and me. But in that moment, the Universe spoke to me, telling me I had a choice: I could continue down my current path, living a life of disappointment and fear; or I could change and, through my new thoughts and beliefs, be my best self and create the life I'd always dreamed of.

At this point, I was considered clinically obese; I was in a great deal of credit-card debt; I was living in an unhealthy environment with people who put me down; and, worst of all, I didn't know how to love myself or my life. That's when I began to read a book by Louise that changed my life forever—*You Can Heal Your Life*. After working my way through the chapters, I went on to find other books, audio programs, and DVDs by Louise. By taking all of these in, along with the great wisdom and love that they contain, I was able to open my eyes and see myself and the world around me in a new light. Through the exercises and beautiful affirmations that Louise offers, I was able to work on releasing many of the old negative beliefs that had been holding me back. I started to love myself and be a deliberate creator of my own existence.

It's now a year later, and I'm proud and so incredibly grateful to report that I'm 60 pounds lighter, and healthier than I've ever been. I'm living in my own beautiful home, I'm free of debt, and I'm more financially stable than I have been in the past. I can say, for the first time ever, that I truly love myself and my life. I also feel that as a result of my new beliefs and attitudes, I'm inclined to touch and uplift those around me. I've passed on Louise's books and wisdom to many loved ones in my life, and they've greatly benefited from her wonderful gifts as well.

Louise, thank you for being you, and for all of the glorious things that you do. Because of you, I know that my journey is just beginning, and I am loving every minute of it!

✗ ✗ ✗

Feeling Alive Again

by Parvin, webmaster, Canada

At age 12, I lost my father; at age 18, I left Iran right after the revolution to go to India; at age 21, I got married; and at age 26, I moved to Canada.

When I left Iran, I was a pretty independent girl, considering the way I was raised and the culture I was brought up in. However, my life turned upside down after I got married. My relationship with my husband was a disaster: I endured constant emotional, physical, and mental abuse; and I gradually lost my self-worth and everything that made me who I was up to that point.

I had my first child in 1985. Although it was a year after I'd moved to Canada, I was still experiencing culture shock, and I hated being away from my family. Thanks to my abusive husband, having a newborn, feeling inexperienced as a mother, and lacking any support in my life, my self-worth was at zero. Many times I wanted to leave, but my low self-esteem didn't allow me to do so. I had my second child four and a half years later, and things got even worse. I gained weight and didn't have the desire to take care of myself in any way.

In 1991 I lost my oldest sister in a car accident, and I wasn't able to go to her funeral because the government in Iran wouldn't let me return to the country. I was so devastated that I cried day and night for months, and my hair started falling out. And even though I gained more weight, I felt like there was basically nothing left of me.

During all of this trauma, I started working as a dental assistant in a small office. One day I saw that the dentist I was working with had a book in her hand with a big rainbow on the cover. The title read: *You Can Heal Your Life*. I asked if I could borrow the book for a few days, and she said yes. I remember when I got home that night, I couldn't wait to put the kids to sleep so I could read. As soon as I started the book, I was sure that it had been written for me. It felt as if someone were pouring nice cool water on the fire raging inside of me. I did the exercises and read every single page; I felt alive again.

I think I went on to read *You Can Heal Your Life* 20 times, and ultimately I was able to stand on my feet again and appreciate myself. After a while, I could actually go to the mirror, look into my eyes, and say "I love you." I found some very good friends, and life started to have some meaning. I thank God for my boss the dentist, and most of all, for Louise Hay. Over the years, I've bought all of Louise's books and CDs—and whenever I find someone who's in the same situation I was in, I give him or her a copy of *You Can Heal Your Life* as a gift from me and Louise.

Louise, I love you with all my heart. Thank you for everything.

꙰ ꙰ ꙰

Blessings for a Safe Trip
by Sandra, office manager, Colorado

One year ago I moved to Fort Collins, Colorado; however, I work 40 miles away in Cheyenne, Wyoming. I'd heard hair-raising stories about the winter weather and how bad the roads could get between the two cities. I started worrying constantly about the weather and was very nervous driving to and from work, and then I read Louise Hay's advice on blessing your trip as well as your car before leaving the house. So that's what I started doing: Now every time I go to work and come home, I bless the car, the weather, and the other drivers on the road. I end by saying, "Thank You, God, for a safe trip."

Here is the miraculous part. In the last year, I've seen ice, snowstorms, gale-force winds, and tornadoes . . . but never when I'm on the road. On my way home from work, I've seen blizzards as I walk out the door, then I turn the corner, and it's clear. One day the wind was blowing more than 50 miles an hour all day; just as I was about to leave, a co-worker went outside and announced that the wind had completely stopped. I just smiled and said, "Thank You, God."

This story might not seem big to some, but all of this has been huge for me. I am truly thankful for the gift Louise gave me and the miracles I've experienced by changing my beliefs and having faith in the power within.

⚹ ⚹ ⚹

My Moment of Clarity
by Rosalyn, local government employee, Florida

For years I had the feeling that I was meant to *be* more and *have* more than my circumstances seemed to allow. I certainly wanted more out of life, but it always seemed that the more I tried, the more I spun my wheels. I always had a good job, although I also just managed to get by. I'd say, "All I want is enough to pay my bills"—and that's exactly what I got.

At one point several years ago I was introduced to Norman Vincent Peale's book *The Power of Positive Thinking.* I understood the words, but what he wrote about seemed hard for me to grasp. Then, about three years ago, I vowed that things were going to change for me. I was willing to do everything I could to make sure of it.

It seemed that once I made the decision that my life would get better, things began to fall right into place. To begin with, I determined that instead of the typical fiction I'd been devouring since I was 12 years old, everything I read from now on would serve to help me become a better person. Yet it wasn't until I was led to Louise Hay's *You Can Heal Your Life* that I had my moment of clarity.

The idea that I had the power to think past my current situation and focus my thoughts on how I wished my life to be intrigued me so much that I decided to put this theory into action. *After all,* I thought, *here's someone who cured herself of cancer. If she could do that, then I ought to be able to change my situation, which isn't nearly as bad.* So I thought about how I wanted my life to be. Slowly, one affirmation at a time, I started to believe that things would change. That's when I really began to enjoy the journey.

When I read "the list" in Louise's book, with its probable causes for particular mind-body issues, I was blown away. I'd been having a problem hearing out of one ear for almost a year. I'd gone to the doctor and tried popping my ear, but nothing helped. Then I thought about a person who was close to me and who had the tendency to speak about every hurt endured in life—it had gotten to the point where I just didn't want to hear about it anymore, so I started to tune it out. That would explain my hearing problem! I began repeating the new thought pattern Louise suggested every day. I tried popping my ear again about a week later, and lo and behold, everything was great. I haven't had a problem with my hearing since . . . and I'm no longer surprised when the things I allow begin showing up in my life.

Thanks to you, Louise, I'm living proof that you really can heal your life.

ⅇ ⅇ ⅇ

I Deserve to Be Happy
by Tamara, spiritual counselor, Arizona

In 1996 I was enrolled at the Swedish Institute in Manhattan, studying to become a massage therapist. I was diagnosed with a couple of autoimmune diseases and told that I had to quit school because massaging would negatively affect my illnesses. I was distraught—I loved being in school and helping others heal.

A friend saw my distress and handed me the book *You Can Heal Your Life,* by Louise Hay. I thought it was mumbo jumbo at first, but the more I read, the more my spirit seemed to lighten. I started using affirmations and even stuck them onto the dashboard of my car. I would cry every time I told myself, *I deserve love,* or *I am perfect exactly as I am.* My head was anxious, but my soul knew the truth.

I'd just left an abusive marriage, and I kept reminding myself, *I deserve to be happy.* Shortly after I got my own place with my kids, my nine-year-old daughter and I were in a horrible car accident, and she died a week later. I clung to my affirmations for dear life, and through even more tears, I worked on forgiving myself.

Over and over again, I told myself, *I deserve to be happy.* My mind didn't want to believe this, but once again, my spirit craved the words and they brought me peace. No matter what was going on or how bad things got—through alcoholism, strained family relationships, and my health issues—I used affirmations to get through my day. And believe me, they worked.

As I sit here today, I've now been in recovery for more than ten years, my family relations are healed, and I have a wonderful life. My favorite affirmation is: *I deserve to give and receive love.* To that end, I've attracted an amazing man into my life who loves *all* of me.

I now run a women's spiritual-empowerment group for addicts, prostitutes, and abused women; and I use Louise's book *Empowering Women* and her DVD of *You Can Heal Your Life* as part of my class. I know from the bottom of my heart that the impact of her work has helped heal my life from one of helplessness to one of hopefulness. All is well in my world!

Thank you, Louise, and God bless the work you have done for me and others.

✍ ✍ ✍

Saving Myself
by Kelly, freelance writer and blogger, Australia

Louise Hay is the closest thing I have to a guru. Her book *You Can Heal Your Life* opened my eyes to a new way of being and gave me a glimpse of who I could become. Quite simply, reading this book changed the course of my life forever.

I was only 20 when my mother gave me Louise's book, and I'd already managed to attract a relationship that was controlling, emotionally abusive, and violent. On the outside I looked like an intelligent, driven young woman with her whole life ahead of her. On the inside, however, I was a screaming and tormented child, raging against abandonment, lost innocence, and the shame of sexual abuse. I desperately wanted to be happy, but the world I lived in was full of pain and criticism. I was trying so hard to be perfect and hating myself because I was not.

As soon as I read Louise's story, it was like the sun came out. All of a sudden, I could see that every day didn't have to be cloudy—there was a blue sky out there! I realized that I had to change myself before I could ever have the life I dreamed of.

I knew that cancer tended to run in one side of my family, and alcoholism and mental disease ran in the other. I didn't want a life that included any of these things, but the signs were already there that addiction and depression were waiting to become close friends of mine. I decided then and there that I would remake myself and my life, and I would transcend everything that had gone on before.

This journey took many years, mostly because it isn't easy to let go of the past. Events may fade from memory, but feelings of loss, rejection, and betrayal tend to hang around and nest in your heart. They clog your arteries and sit heavily on your chest, so you feel like you're drowning in the ugliness that your life has been.

I had to choose to change, and part of that was letting go of the past and the comfort of my pain. Yes, I had every reason to be angry at the world—I'd had crappy luck and deserved better. But Louise made me see that the only one who was going to give me a better life was *me*. I had to save myself.

I was lucky enough to meet and speak with Louise after a seminar in Sydney in 1995, and I will never forget the light that shone out from this woman. She was incandescent, like an angel, which is fitting. After all, what I learned from Louise is that I am also a living, breathing angel who deserves unconditional love and acceptance. I am worthy of the best that life has to offer, and I love myself exactly as I am.

Louise Lends a Hand
by Linda, lightworker and Realtor, California

In the early 1980s I found Louise Hay's "little blue book," *Heal Your Body,* at the Bodhi Tree Bookstore in Los Angeles. I was delighted and amazed to have come upon such a resource. I was able to contact Louise and tell her about the work I was doing with convicts in maximum-security prisons.

Louise graciously gave me 100 copies of *Heal Your Body* to send to prisoners across America. The men were thrilled to receive the books, and even passed them on to the chaplains and the prison libraries. I'm certain that the light multiplied exponentially and continues to do so!

A few years later I took my mother to see Louise, who was doing private consultations at the time, to help her with her own life issues. I told her, "Mom, this lady is not from here. She just came to the planet to lend a hand." I visited with Louise's own mother while mine was having a treatment, and it was very lovely.

As we left Louise's beautiful Santa Monica home, I asked my mom, "Well, what did you think?" She beamed and sweetly said, "You're right! Louise is not from here! She must have just come to lend a hand!"

Over the years I've shared Louise's books and ideas with many. I was thrilled to see her movie recently, and I think it will have an even greater impact on the planet than *The Secret* has. Louise is a pioneer, and I feel very fortunate to have met her and been blessed by her teachings and her presence. As a woman, she is an inspiration; as a business leader and a lightworker, she is brilliant!

Lifted into the Heavens

by Pamila Faye, feng-shui practitioner, Virginia

In 1996 a friend gave me a copy of *Heal Your Body,* and I was shocked by the truth and accuracy behind the mind-body connection. Then in 1999 my life had an explosion: my husband of 20 years was caught in an affair and subsequently left me; my eldest child, who was a senior in high school, got pregnant and wanted to marry the young man whom her father had forbidden her to see for a year before this; and I was diagnosed with stage III cervical cancer. I hit bottom and needed to find a way to look up.

Over the years that followed, I read several of Louise's books, and each one helped me to heal. My favorite one came on a day I was lower than I'd ever been, and I'd gone to the bookstore to find something to help me. I asked the Universe for guidance in finding the right book, and there it was: *Gratitude,* by Louise Hay.

When I got home, I sat right down and read every story. This book lifted me into the heavens, and I realized from all these people's stories that everything would work out for me, I had nothing to fear, and all I needed to do was love and trust myself. The Universe would deliver whatever I desired, and it would all be fine. That afternoon I sent out my desires, put on my favorite outfit and favorite music, and poured my soul into the moment. I immediately felt much better. It wasn't long before the serious problem that had led me to *Gratitude* that day in the bookstore was settled— so beautifully settled, in fact, that I couldn't have imagined such a wonderful conclusion!

I've since bought that book dozens of times for friends and family members, asking them to read at least a story a day when they're feeling hopeless and in despair. And they've all told me how it has helped them!

Louise, thank you for sharing all the truth you've learned in life. I am forever grateful, and hope to meet you soon so I can give you a big hug!

ϰ ϰ ϰ

The Louise Revolution!

by Bayleigh, insurance agent, Indiana

I first saw Louise Hay on *Oprah* in 2008. I had just been fired from a job where I'd been miserable, was surrounded by negative influences, and was lonely and sad. I watched the episode and immediately ordered *You Can Heal Your Life*. In the meantime, I had taken notes while viewing the show and was determined to change my life. I created a vision board and started saying affirmations right away.

I'm amazed at all I've experienced in the past six months. I've found my spirituality again, and I have a true relationship with God. I am also working my way out of financial debt. Being positive kept me above water during the four months it took to get another job, and I did find a new career that I enjoy. I reconnected with my first love, and we are engaged to be married this October. (I'd previously resolved to be single for the rest of my life.) My fiancé also read *You Can Heal Your Life* and is becoming a strong man after years of being a doormat. (I told him that I wouldn't marry anyone who refused to read the book or live by it. He was hesitant at first, but is living it now!)

My fiancé has two young children. We bought them Louise's books for Christmas, and they're learning to do affirmations every day and understanding that they can *choose* to be positive. We see improvement in the kids all the time, and are excited to know that their lives will be enriched at such an early age.

I've told everyone I know to get *You Can Heal Your Life* and stop making excuses for the problems in their lives. Today my mom, sister, and aunt are a part of the Louise revolution as well! I feel like I know Louise and that she is a beautiful guiding light in my life. I loved her movie, and I listen to her affirmation CDs whenever I need a boost. Something good always happens after that "refresher."

Louise, I am so thankful for you. I am now a *very* happy woman, and my life gets more fabulous every day!

✿ ✿ ✿

Already Being

by Susan, bartender, human-resources specialist, notary . . .
just to name a few, Massachusetts

I remember one Thanksgiving Day when I was five or six years old and my aunt asked me what I wanted to be when I grew up. With a look of bafflement, I responded, "I'm already being." I went on to explain that I'd still be me even when I grew up. My aunt, looking equally as baffled, was at a loss for words.

Of course, as time went by I eventually realized what she was asking . . . and as my occupations above indicate, I've "become" quite a few things. But the truth for me is that the gifts, talents, thoughts, and so forth required to "occupy" my time were already there when I was born. It's just societal beliefs that require a title for each occupation. I could add mother, daughter, sister, and wife, too—but, again, the ability to have these roles was already there as part of my being.

When I first read Louise's book *You Can Heal Your Life* back in 1984, I was 28 years old. I remember thinking, *Now there's someone who knows how I feel. Louise would know exactly what I mean by "I'm already being"!* By this point, I'd allowed myself to take on many societal beliefs about myself that simply weren't true. For example, I was a buxom, blue-eyed blonde, which meant that my only roles were to be dumb and sexy. Reading Louise's book was the start of letting go of the many false beliefs I carried with me. Once I understood where or who each belief came from, I was able to let it go, realizing that it wasn't my belief in the first place.

It's a wonderful miracle to be able to just change your thought, and in that instant, your life is changed. And the change is always for the better because you're replacing a negative thought with a positive one.

Thank you, dear Louise, for sharing your thoughts with all of us. They have put me back on the path of simply "being"! I send you lots of hugs and happiness.

✒ ✒ ✒

Help from Heaven

by Alena, working, the Netherlands

I am from the Czech Republic, born under communism. My dad is quite despotic and negative—he never told me he loved me or showed any affection. He was also very critical, so it seemed that whatever I did, it was never correct. He thought this behavior would make me strong. It did not. As soon as I graduated from school, I went to work in another city in my country. Then at age 20, I moved to Holland to start a new life.

A friend came with me, and we briefly found work and got a flat. But at that time Czech people were not able to work legally in the Netherlands, so we ended up on the street, living in squalor with weird people, and taking drugs. But we didn't want to go back to our families because of our fathers (hers was even worse than mine).

We regularly walked around the streets to look at what people had thrown away to determine if we could use or sell it. I love books, so whenever I'd see one lying on the ground, I'd grab it. And one day, there was *You Can Heal Your Life*. It actually caught my attention because of the colored cover, which, frankly, I didn't like. Back then, I didn't like colors—my color was black. That's the magic of this story. I found this book on the ground, in the garbage, and I didn't like the cover; still, I took it with me and read it.

Then I went to visit my boyfriend in Ireland, but things didn't work out. I wanted to return to the Netherlands, but due to immigration issues, I was deported back to the Czech Republic. I was terribly upset and called my brother, who was very nice and let me stay at his place for a month.

This was my help from heaven—if I hadn't been deported, I never would have started living like a normal person, loving myself, and appreciating who I am. I am now 29 and back in Holland, but this time I work in an office and live in a nice flat. It is my dream to teach kindergarten. I know that I'm meant to spend time with children and teach them things that are really important, such as how to love others and themselves.

I came to realize that I don't need to have my father telling me how great I am. Of course I'd love to hear something positive from him, but I know that he's doing his best. I love all of my family members very much and am so happy to have them in my life. This year we will spend our first Christmas together in many years, which is wonderful.

Now things are great. Even if tough things happen, I know that this is just a lesson for me and to take it as a test. I love being in this school of life!

I love you, dear Louise, and I wish you all the best in everything. You are an angel to me and have really helped me heal my life. (By the way, I love all the colors of the rainbow now!)

꒰ ꒰ ꒰

A Sonnet for Louise
by Laurie, attorney, Indiana

I was born into a zero-sum world, where each of us competes for limited resources, and the only way for one to win is for another to lose. In that world, *masculine* means "powerful" and *feminine* means "weak." Children are to be seen and not heard; women are to submit and obey. For years I struggled to break free from that oppressive world, never realizing that the oppression came from my own self-defeating belief systems. I studied law and learned to be assertive, but no matter what I achieved, I was still destined to fail. I'd always be a woman trying to succeed in a man's world.

All of that changed when I began reading Louise Hay's books. As I learned to love myself and use positive affirmations, every day became a miracle. I'm now raising my daughter in an abundant world, where each of us has everything she needs and enough to share with others. In our world, *masculine* and *feminine* are valued equally and embraced fully as complementary parts of humanity. Children are acknowledged, cherished, and encouraged to think for themselves. Love and kindness have replaced fear and manipulation. Cooperation replaces competition. Life is good; it's *all* good.

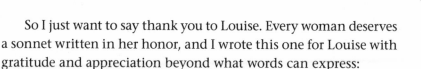
So I just want to say thank you to Louise. Every woman deserves a sonnet written in her honor, and I wrote this one for Louise with gratitude and appreciation beyond what words can express:

To think that I can learn to love myself,
To know that wisdom comes to those who wait,
To nurture body, mind, and soul to health,
And tell myself each moment, "I am great!"

My life reflects beliefs held in my heart.
I change my world each time I change my mind.
Acceptance is the only place to start,
And I achieve success by being kind.

Each morning I wake up and I affirm,
"Everything I need today is mine."
Prosperity awaits at every turn.
The Universe's timing is Divine.

I always will be grateful to Ms. Hay
For showing me this kinder, gentler way.

Doing the Work with Louise

What do you want to change in your own life? Do you know which of your thought patterns are contributing to the unwanted situation? However long you've held on to these beliefs, understand that they no longer support you, and it is okay to let them go now. You *can* manifest a new future for yourself, one filled with joy and love.

When you feel ready to start the mental work, the following exercises will help you examine your beliefs in-depth. After all, you can't begin to transform your old beliefs if you don't even know what they are! (Do be sure to write your answers on a separate piece of paper or in your journal.)

Discovering Your Beliefs

Think of all the beliefs that the words in the list below bring to your mind. Feel free to add more categories in other areas of your life that are not working well. Make the list as long as you like. Write everything down—both your positive and negative beliefs— so that you can see your thoughts clearly. These are the internal, subconscious rules you live your life by. Remember that you cannot make positive changes in your life until you can recognize the beliefs you currently hold.

- Men
- Women
- Love
- Sex
- Work
- Money
- Success
- Failure
- God

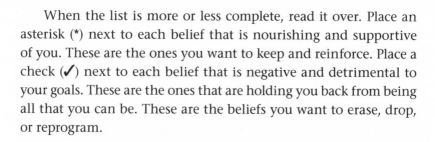

When the list is more or less complete, read it over. Place an asterisk (*) next to each belief that is nourishing and supportive of you. These are the ones you want to keep and reinforce. Place a check (✓) next to each belief that is negative and detrimental to your goals. These are the ones that are holding you back from being all that you can be. These are the beliefs you want to erase, drop, or reprogram.

Negative Messages

Next, list all the things your parents said were "wrong" with you. What were the negative messages you heard? Give yourself enough time to remember as many as you can. A half hour usually works well.

What did they say about money? What did they say about your body? What did they say about love and relationships? What did they say about your creative talents? What were the limiting or negative things they said to you?

If you can, just look objectively at your list and say to yourself, "So *that's* where that belief came from."

Now let's dig a little deeper. What other negative messages did you hear as a child? What were you told by relatives, teachers, friends, authority figures, or clergy members? Write them all down. Take your time. Be aware of the feelings going on in your body as you do so.

What you have now is another list of thoughts that need to be removed from your consciousness. These are more beliefs that are making you feel "not good enough."

Your Story

Write a brief story of your life, beginning with your childhood. Take care to mention any changes in your emotions or behavior. What negative beliefs could you have in your subconscious mind? Allow them to come up. You may be surprised by what you find.

How many negative messages did you notice when you wrote your story? Treat each one that surfaced as a treasure: "Aha! I've found you. You're the one that has been causing me all this trouble. Now I can eliminate you and be free."

This would be a good time to go to the mirror, look in your eyes, and affirm your willingness to release all these old negative messages and beliefs. Breathe deeply as you do so, and say: *"I am willing to release negative concepts and beliefs that no longer nourish me."* Repeat this several times.

Replacing Your "Shoulds"

As I've said many times, I believe that *should* is one of the most damaging words in our language. Every time we use it, we are, in effect, saying that we *are* wrong, or we *were* wrong, or we're *going to be* wrong. I would like to take the word *should* out of our vocabulary forever and replace it with the word *could*. This word gives us a choice, and then we're never wrong.

Think of five things that you "should" do, and write them down. Then rewrite those statements, replacing *should* with *could*.

Now, ask yourself, "Why haven't I?" You may find that you've been berating yourself for years for something that you never wanted to do in the first place, or for something that was never your idea.

How many "shoulds" can you drop from your list? Write down how this makes you feel.

Fears and Affirmations

For each category listed on the next page, write down your greatest fear. Then place a positive affirmation that would counteract that fear next to it. Create your own, or use one of those that follow.

- Career
- Living situation
- Family relations
- Money
- Physical appearance
- Sex
- Health
- Relationships
- Old age
- Death and dying

Affirmations

I believe in my own power to change.

I am at peace with all of life.

This is a new moment. I am free to let go.

I am willing to forgive all those who have harmed me.

I take responsibility for my own life.

I am willing to create new thoughts for myself and my life.

I am one with the Power that created me. All is well in my world.

I see myself in a new light. I love myself.

I move forward, free from the past. I am safe.

It is safe for me to move beyond others' limitations.

I trust the process of life.

I am open and willing to change.

I recognize that I am the source of my happiness.

I release that which no longer serves me.

I am open and receptive to wonderful, good experiences coming into my life.

I go beyond limiting beliefs and accept myself totally.

I claim my own power and lovingly create my own reality.

I am willing to release all old negative concepts and beliefs that are no longer supporting me.

I am at peace with myself and my life.

I forgive and release the past. I move into joy.

Treatment for Transforming Old Beliefs

*My life is ever new. Each moment of my life is fresh and vital. I
use my affirmative thinking to create exactly what I want. This is
a new day. I am a new me. I think differently. I speak differently. I act
differently. Others treat me differently. My new world is a reflection
of my new thinking. It is a joy and a delight to plant new seeds,
for I know these seeds will become my new experiences.
All is well in my world.*

Chapter Ten

Finding Purpose

We all go through periods where we wonder how we'll ever achieve our life's purpose, or whether we even <u>have</u> a purpose. It might feel like something is missing, and we don't know how to fill that void. Some of us may turn to drugs, unhealthy relationships, or other self-destructive behaviors in an attempt to give our lives meaning. Perhaps we believe that we don't have the right to ask for more or feel like there isn't anything more than what we can see in front of us. But each of us <u>does</u> deserve the best that life has to offer.

Changing your mind is the first step to manifesting your best life. Remember that happiness isn't something that can be found "out there"; it can only come from within, through self-love and acceptance. Learn to love yourself and trust the Divine intelligence within you. The Universe will bring you what you need if you simply allow it.

I hope that the following stories of others finding meaning in their lives will inspire <u>you</u> to see the greater purpose in your own life and motivate you to realize your full potential.

A Passionate, Purposeful Life

by Sharon, author, international speaker,
and producer, California

I have danced with life and death throughout my existence. I overcame nine years of sexual abuse as a child; and I survived bouts with anorexia, several destructive relationships, and two suicide attempts as an adult.

I saw myself as a victim until 1985. That's when I met my mentor, Linda, who worked with me on my feelings of self-hatred, anger, fear, and resentment. Linda gave me a copy of Louise Hay's book *You Can Heal Your Life,* and I went through all the exercises in its pages: I began using affirmations, which resonated with me; did visualizations; and started doing mirror work, telling myself, "I love you, Sharon. I really love you." Louise's book also helped me work on my core issues such as forgiveness, gratitude, relationships, and health.

Before long I understood how powerful my thoughts and words were in association with my health and well-being. I learned all I could about the mind-body-spirit connection and came to feel and experience inner peace, empowerment, and forgiveness for myself and others. I also learned to embrace a positive attitude, regardless of my circumstances.

In 1986 I started volunteering in the AIDS and cancer communities, teaching the mind-body-spirit techniques I'd learned. I also taught classes at juvenile halls and at a correctional facility for teenage girls. Late that year, I faced another challenge when I saw my ex-husband on a Dan Rather television special, "AIDS Hits Home," in which he announced that he was infected with AIDS. I was tested, and the tests were positive for HIV. Yet I allowed the virus to empower me rather than identify me as a helpless victim— I became one of the first infected women in Southern California to go public.

I began attending Louise's Hayride support group for gay men infected with HIV and AIDS. (I believe I was the first heterosexual infected woman who attended.) Louise and the men were filled with compassion, love, gratitude, and a zest for life; and I felt part

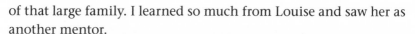

of that large family. I learned so much from Louise and saw her as another mentor.

In 1997 I had a near-death experience due to AIDS complications. I was told that it wasn't my time to die yet and was given my life purpose. I understood that each challenge I faced seeded the gifts and wisdom I could share with others.

By embracing all of my challenges and releasing them, they've become sacred—because they've healed me, brought me to self-discovery, restored me to wholeness, and allowed me to live my life purpose with passion. Now I'm sharing the knowledge and wisdom I've amassed from Louise in my books and with my audiences in the United States, Canada, Europe, Japan, and Russia. Louise is a gift to humanity and a blessing in my life! She is a pioneer and legend. Her legacy will live on forever!

Louise, from the center of my heart, I honor you. You are so deeply loved!

ⵈ ⵈ ⵈ

My Path Was Suddenly Clear
by Antoinette, psychotherapist, yoga and meditation
teacher, and author, Canada

I lived through a civil war in Lebanon. At the age of 13, I was trained by one of the militia factions and became a civil soldier. In horror, I witnessed what human beings are capable of doing. This was not happening in the movies—it was real. My brother was shot and wounded in front of my eyes. I wanted to stay and fight, but my family decided to leave Lebanon and go to Canada to help my brother.

When I was in college, I started feeling that I had to make a change in the world. My background was one of war, so I didn't know how to participate in peaceful politics. Then a person very dear to me drowned—my whole world collapsed and my foundation cracked. I finished my studies in psychology, just searching for a light. After all I'd been through, I couldn't understand how human beings could be so loving and also so destructive.

Sometime later I discovered the books of Louise Hay in French. What a gift! As I read them, these books made me realize that no matter how we're living—whatever our background or even physical state may be—we can transform it. My path was suddenly clear with the new light I received.

I'm now a psychotherapist, a yoga and meditation teacher, and a leader of conferences and workshops. I also recently wrote a book that was published in French, and I hope it will come out in English so I can offer it to Louise! It guides people to liberate themselves from their inner wars and then create a world of love for themselves and the individuals around them. I hope to see the world in peace one day, and I know that the path is through love!

All of my work these days is meant to make the world a better place. I even created two plays in order to portray the potential of the human being. I'm so blessed to be where I am and to do the things that I'm able to do. I think that if all of us work to positively change ourselves, this is the path to changing the world.

Louise, you are an inspiration and a light for the entire planet. Thank you for being who you are and sharing your wisdom with all of us. I sincerely hope that life showers you with all of its most precious gifts. Your books have made me believe in the miracle of love!

※ ※ ※

Stepping-stones to an Amazing Life
by Gina, massage therapist, Massachusetts

When I first found Louise Hay's book *You Can Heal Your Life* in 1999, I was caught up in a whirlwind of anxiety and fear. My negative emotions were making me an angry and impatient mother to my two small boys, and a critical and withdrawn wife to a wonderful, loving husband. I knew I was spiraling out of control, but I felt that I couldn't tell anyone because I was ashamed.

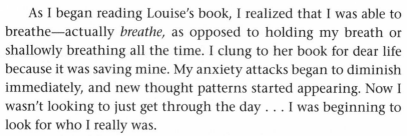

As I began reading Louise's book, I realized that I was able to breathe—actually *breathe*, as opposed to holding my breath or shallowly breathing all the time. I clung to her book for dear life because it was saving mine. My anxiety attacks began to diminish immediately, and new thought patterns started appearing. Now I wasn't looking to just get through the day . . . I was beginning to look for who I really was.

As I was gaining control of my thoughts, I was releasing the need for fear and anxiety, and attracting all the support and guidance I needed to learn about who I was and wanted to become. I knew I was here on this earth to help people—I'd known this from a very young age. Now I was ready to find out *how* I was to help them.

I remember feeling frustrated that things weren't happening fast enough. I wanted everything now! But as I look back, I can see all the stepping-stones quite clearly, one laid out after another on my path. For example, I quit my job and went to massage school. This was an intensive three-month program and I'd only come home for a few nights each week, yet my husband and boys totally supported me.

After I graduated, it took a while before I found a massage job because I had the confidence to be selective, as well as the wisdom not to settle for anything less than what I had envisioned. I practiced under the wing of a very talented massage therapist for a year and became clear about what I wanted. Then in 2007 I was ready to leave the nest and opened my own practice. Today I'm helping numerous people find relief from their physical discomfort—I'm also able to help them realize that their bodies can heal themselves, and that they can heal their lives. . . .

The best part of this experience is that my boys have witnessed all of it. They've seen me grow and step out of my comfort zones and make gigantic leaps of faith. Out of everything that I could have possibly given them in life, I'm grateful that this is what they've received. (In putting my experience into words now, I realized how much easier it is to just be me than it was to run and hide from who I am or be what I thought everyone else may have wanted me to be.)

Louise, I must have read *You Can Heal Your Life* hundreds of times, and I've bought many of your books to hand out to friends and relatives. Thank you so much for everything.

≮ ≮ ≮

Celebrating My Bliss
by Bianca Maria, life coach and artist, Ireland

My story begins 26 years ago in Germany. Tormented by a violent and abusive upbringing, I barely experienced love in any way. With an alcoholic mother and a father who left us when I was really young, I struggled through my childhood in a lot of pain.

Thanks to my shattered self-esteem and lack of positive energy, I grew up to be an extremely jealous person, and nothing really worked in my life. Yet ever since I was little, I've always had a huge connection to my higher self and to nature, which soothed my soul and helped me survive.

I left home when I was 16 years old and started to work in a hotel. It was quite challenging because I knew absolutely nothing about manners—or life at all, for that matter. My journey of healing began in earnest when I moved to Ireland. Trying to work through my tremendous fears and limitations, I went to an Al-Anon meeting, where friends, relatives, children, or spouses of alcoholics could find great support.

At one of these meetings I met a woman who introduced me to Louise Hay. After reading Louise's amazing book *You Can Heal Your Life,* I felt that I had the strength to look inside myself and change my life. I began the process by writing at least three pages of affirmations a day! I thought that if affirmations really did work, then these pages were creating a wonderful future for me . . . and that's exactly what they did.

Within three months I was able to bring my pathological jealousy down to a manageable level, and I discovered a gathering of like-minded spiritual people in my town. After about six months, lots of little miracles happened! I attracted a wonderful relationship, some lovely new friends, and a lot more money. I also lost almost 30 pounds and started meditating every day.

It's been two years now since I first started practicing the work of Louise, and my life is still unfolding in the most perfect way! I started a "You Can Heal Your Life" meeting in my living room, where we help each other face-to-face. Creating my own Website, along with a group on the Internet to support women around the world, has given me the opportunity to spread Louise's message even more. Proudly, I can now say that I know I'm a born teacher, chosen to help others heal and create the life they really deserve. I feel I've found my life's purpose!

Today I'm grateful for my childhood, for it made me the beautiful person I am. Life has gone on to become exciting, special, and loving for me—I continue on my path by exploring different viewpoints and teachers, learning the lessons I came here to learn. This is bliss, and I celebrate it!

Louise, you are an angel to me, and I have so much appreciation for all you've done. You've changed the world for the better—you've given lots of love to many people who felt lost or not good enough, and who were in deep pain and fear. Thank you so very much!

✘ ✘ ✘

I Can Fly
by Gail, singer, speaker, writer, and teacher, Colorado

In 1987 I had Louise Hay's book *You Can Heal Your Life* put into braille for me, and my fingers have glided over its pages countless times. She didn't cure me from cancer or any other physical disease, but she healed the disease that was in my mind.

Before I read Louise's book, I was a victim. Born prematurely, I believed that my limitations were the fault of doctors, as well as because of my mother's drinking and smoking. I grew up withdrawn, angry, fearful, and disconnected. After undergoing two nose operations, I remember looking into the mirror and thinking, *You're ugly. I hate you.* I was abused by my father and totally blind at age 11 as a result of cataracts. I had nothing to look forward to, so I closed my eyes to the world, not wanting to be a part of it.

My grandmother and my music were my saving graces. Grandma provided love and hope, while my music grounded me to the present and allowed me to express myself. Leaving my parents' home, I embarked on a career as a concert singer. After scores of successful performances, I entered a doctorate program in voice. I wanted to sing and make beautiful music, but the school's staff "clipped my wings." My creativity stifled, I developed an ovarian cyst that had to be surgically removed.

My life hit rock bottom when my romantic relationship crumbled. I'd given up my music, dreams, and autonomy in the hopes of being loved. I was now incapable of making decisions, stating my needs, saying no, or speaking my truth. Having given away my body, mind, spirit, and emotions, when my life partner announced a "separation," I was devastated. With no reconciliation in sight, I became depressed and suicidal.

Through psychotherapy I began to heal and to love myself, and I discovered that I had a reason for being. I wanted to tell my story and speak my truth. So I chronicled how, within a three-month span, my mother suddenly died, I had a hysterectomy, I had both my eyes removed, and I had to sell my house. As I let go of my old beliefs, visions, and connections, I was forced to embrace the new.

Thanks to my life's journey—and reading *You Can Heal Your Life*—I've learned to speak my truth, face my fears, and feel my feelings. Now my desire to fly is bigger than my fear of falling. I have a choice in how I look at life: I can be paralyzed and victimized by my circumstances, or I can be empowered by them. I choose the latter. Vision is internal, not external, and it's guided by my heart, not my eyes. In order to fly, I have to "live my dreams, and fly on my wings."

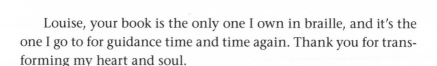

Louise, your book is the only one I own in braille, and it's the one I go to for guidance time and time again. Thank you for transforming my heart and soul.

ɤ ɤ ɤ

The Revelation

by Najmunesa, parenting coach, trainer/facilitator,
and spiritual counselor, South Africa

When I first came across the book *You Can Heal Your Life,* I was at a very low point in my life. The youngest of 16 children, I've always felt like the black sheep of the family. I mean this literally: I grew up in the dark days of apartheid, and I wasn't as light skinned as the rest of my siblings. I felt that my mother hated me, and I was constantly acting out in order to be noticed and have a feeling of belonging.

I burst a blood vessel in the right side of my brain when I gave birth to my first child, but this didn't get diagnosed until years later. I suffered epileptic fits and postpartum depression, and developed a hyperactive thyroid. After my second child I had a nervous breakdown, which in later years I'd view as a break*through* instead of a break*down.*

I found a copy of Louise's book in the library, but it took me many years to read it. I learned about her "Heal Your Life" workshops, but they were only offered to whites. My boss at the time felt that I was "white enough" and took me to one of them. I attended each and every one of these workshops over the years, and that's how my life changed. At the same time I enrolled in a course on spirituality, and I was amazed by the correlation between my faith and Louise's premises. The experience was truly a revelation. I learned that I could retain my values, even as I worked on changing my beliefs.

Today I work in grassroots communities, facilitating parenting and self-awareness workshops. I'm the coordinator for a group that helps people with depression and anxiety, and I used to be the hotline counselor as well. Louise's work changed my life and helped me find my way, and I now try to do the same for others. Thank you for affording me the opportunity to share my story.

❦ ❦ ❦

My Motivation and Inspiration
by Lourdes, bilingual case manager/social services, Arizona

I came to the United States from Sonora, Mexico, in 1993. I spoke no English at all and had left behind the most precious treasures of my life: my two daughters, who were eight and three at the time. Three months later my girls and I were reunited, and we began to adjust to our new world.

In a year I'd met a wonderful American man who wrapped my daughters and me in his love, kindness, and acceptance. Despite our language barrier, we developed a close relationship. When we didn't understand each other, we utilized a Spanish-to-English dictionary. We got married and have been a family for 14 years now.

I cleaned houses for many years, making a decent living out of it. I eventually enrolled in college; although I didn't graduate, I did learn English and majored in social work. I went on to work in a hospital as a certified medical interpreter. Yet I suffered from anxiety attacks and felt as if I'd lost my way.

As part of my daily life, I got into yoga, running, tai chi, and hiking. I attended several self-help seminars, learned about meditation, and much more. Thanks to all of these new experiences I was having, so many issues began to unravel within me. I realized that there were things I didn't like about myself and that I wanted to change. I began to work on the puzzle of my life: where I came from; the environment I'd grown up in; my beliefs, habits, behavior, and feelings; and so forth.

At one of the seminars I attended, I heard about Susan Jeffers's book *Feel the Fear . . . and Do It Anyway*. This book was the key that started the motor in my being. In it, I found out about Louise Hay and *You Can Heal Your Life*, along with the titles of so many other books and wonderful authors. Yet it's Louise's work that has been my motivation all of these years. I love her story, her advice, her courage . . . I could go on and on with the list. Thanks to her audio program *Stress-Free,* I've been able to manage my anxieties and fears. The music on it helped me travel into a spiritual, safe, and peaceful place.

Because of Louise, I was inspired to write and publish my own self-help autobiography in Spanish. It has been utilized to uplift and empower Latina women in the community who are involved in domestic violence or who have low self-esteem, doubts, and fear. These women have identified with my story during my volunteer services as a motivational Spanish speaker, just as I identified with Louise's.

I'm now 41 years old, and my daughters are 24 and 18 and doing wonderfully. All three of us are American citizens and proudly contributing to this country. I feel that we're healthy women, physically, mentally, and emotionally. My marriage continues to grow with peace and love. My inner child has bloomed to its fullest potential, singing and writing as I once did when I was a little girl.

Thank you so much, Louise!

❦ ❦ ❦

Louise's Wisdom
by Pamina, life coach and stress-management consultant, Zimbabwe

Louise Hay's *You Can Heal Your Life* was sent to me by an Australian friend 13 years ago, at a time when my life wasn't looking too promising. In this BL (Before Louise) period, I was weighed down by the kind of emotional baggage that would kill an elephant, wore historical scars and limiting labels as though they were a much-sought-after fashion accessory, and had a self-image that would have made an anorexic earthworm seem impressive. Louise's book turned the world as I'd known it upside down. I played a part in all this? I created my reality? That means I have the power to rewrite this dismal life script? Could I really be that powerful? Wow! What a lightbulb moment!

AL (After Louise), her wisdom was my constant companion. I still have my original dog-eared, glued-together copy of *You Can Heal Your Life;* its ripple effect has spread far and wide. I learned to live solo and love it. I stopped allowing myself to be enslaved by my history and defined by my failures. I quit fighting ghosts. The complexity of my problems no longer held any allure. I became more fearless by the day. I ceased getting satisfaction out of the garbage-groping, pain-probing anger orgies and poor-me purges that had become such a part of my life. My desire for blame binges and self-torture triathlons waned. In other words, I outgrew my self-obsession and began to become emotionally mature. I let go of my hard-earned material possessions and became a nomad, seeking enabling environments for my sojourn of self-rediscovery.

Louise's wisdom and strength were there when I buried my 16-year-old daughter. One painful step at a time, I climbed out of that deep, dark pit where I lay feeling as though I'd been disemboweled. And I was also able to then help my teenage son survive while he battled bereavement, blame, and frustration.

I always travel light, but you can be sure that Louise's "book of wisdom" is tucked away in my bag. The essence of its guidance was there by my side when I successfully qualified as a corporate and personal stress-management consultant in a country as foreign to me as Mars. I subsequently went on to become a life coach and hypnotherapist and returned to my troubled homeland, Zimbabwe, to practice on the front lines.

Louise's principles are second nature to me now, as natural as breathing. Like Louise, I'm passionate about helping people transcend their environment, empower themselves, and become the best they can be. It was her example that encouraged me to write my own book, keeping my spirits buoyant enough to ride the inevitable waves of rejection that go with the publishing territory.

Louise, your spirit and wisdom have enabled me to rewrite my life script in miraculous ways. Thank you!

꿏 꿏 꿏

Living the Life of My Dreams
by Kit, teacher, laughter leader, and health-
creation mentor, United Kingdom

Until I encountered Louise Hay in her book *You Can Heal Your Life,* I was oblivious to the power we all have to create our own lives.

In January 1998 my life was a virtual write-off. My superficially picture-perfect marriage was an ugly battleground, my son was in crisis, and I wasn't doing too well myself.

My doctor had told me, "Well, the cancer's back. It's still the same aggressive beast we've been dealing with, and now there are only two chemo drugs that you haven't had the limit of. If they work, it's just about extending your life. If they don't, I promise you that I won't let you suffer, Kit."

At that point I finally stopped being the model patient. "I'm not going along with this," I replied. "I want a miracle."

They say that when you're ready, the teacher will come. I have no idea why I was in the bookstore that day, but I remember the big bright heart and the words *You Can Heal Your Life* drawing me in like a magnet. I bought the book, read it, and reread it. It went on to become part of my life.

For three years Louise's book was constantly with me. I kept one copy on my desk and one beside my bed and read at least one chapter a day. I also repeated the affirmations out loud whenever I needed comfort or inspiration. (Even today I can cope with anything by affirming: *In the infinity of life where I am, all is perfect, whole, and complete.*) Slowly I began to change my thoughts, and my life changed accordingly.

In March 1998 I set myself three seemingly impossible goals:

1. To pull off a miracle
2. To sort out my marriage
3. To quit smoking

By August, I'd given up cancer, marriage, and smoking! Believe it or not, smoking was the last to go—I kept puffing away, even through every chemo treatment, to the despair of my doctors. But

I finally gave up cigarettes. Going through a divorce was probably not the obvious time to try to quit, but it worked for me.

To the mystification of my doctors, I am alive and living the life of my dreams. I'm now happily married to the original love of my life, and my beloved son has grown into a man I respect and is flourishing on his chosen path. I am a Louise Hay "Love Yourself, Heal Your Life" teacher as well as a laughter leader and health-creation mentor. I joyfully teach others to create the life of *their* dreams. In 2007 my first book was published and I'm working on my second. It's wonderful to be alive, contributing to the healing of the planet!

↯ ↯ ↯

Why *Not* Me?
by Janet, program coordinator for
a youth treatment center, Canada

I am a First Nations woman from Canada who's experienced a lengthy series of personal and painful experiences, such as abusive and codependent relationships, drug and alcohol addictions, and thoughts of suicide. Many times throughout my life I felt like a victim and wondered, *Why me?*

I was at a particularly low point in my life when I came across a pamphlet with information about a two-day workshop called "Love Yourself, Heal Your Life." I knew then that this was just what I'd been looking for, and I immediately signed up to attend.

The workshop was amazing, and I learned so much about myself—including how much I disapproved of myself. I ultimately came to the realization that I can love and accept myself just the way I am! Once that happened, everything else in my life started to fall into place.

I took those first steps to discover who I was and why I was the way I was. By practicing the concepts of Louise Hay and by using positive affirmations, I'm happy to report that I do love and accept myself exactly the way I am. I gained a deeper understanding of myself, and instead of wondering, *Why me?* I began to ask, *Why not me?*

In 2002, I learned about a training program in Florida—I was determined to attend, but for a variety of reasons, I wasn't able to do so at that time. However, I kept affirming: *I am a certified "Heal Your Life" workshop leader.* In April 2008, I had the opportunity to take the training in Florida, and I returned back to Canada as a certified "Heal Your Life, Achieve Your Dreams" workshop leader.

It was a dream come true for me because my goal is to help others through motivational training, seminars, workshops, and presentations. Since receiving my certification, I've begun to realize that goal by hosting the first workshop in my community. Seven participants from three different First Nations communities attended, and it was an enormous success.

It was interesting to learn that out of thousands of people trained all over the world, I am actually the only aboriginal person in Canada to take this training and become certified. I am confident that through my workshops I can empower others to overcome the negative mind-set that has limited their success.

What can I dream of next? Meeting Louise Hay, Wayne Dyer, or Oprah in person? Hmm . . .

꙳ ꙳ ꙳

Shining My Own Light
by Eileen, practitioner of the healing arts, North Carolina

I'd like to share my story so I can inspire others to overcome their life challenges, as I have. You see, I suffered from fibromyalgia for more than seven years, to the point that I had constant pain and couldn't even get out of bed. It wasn't until I found spirituality from within and Louise Hay's books that I truly understood what it takes to heal the mind-body-spirit.

Using an intensive program of affirmations, visualization, nutritional cleansing, and psychotherapy, I was able to shed "the layers" that had me in their grip. I moved from fibromyalgia controlling my life to taking the control back myself and embracing my true essence. As my path shifted, I completely healed from my condition and freed myself to find my inner spirit. This enabled me to become self-empowered and to work on healing all aspects of my soul. My health improved, both in mind and body, and my uplifted spirit now knew no limits. My life changed for the better, and I learned to see the world in a much different way—one that is both enlightening and fulfilling.

Louise's healing message was a breath of fresh air and an opportunity for me to realize that I too have a light to shine. Since she made a difference in my life, I felt responsible to continue the thread by making a difference in someone else's life. I found my purpose and now share my own knowledge and wisdom with those who wish to fulfill their own life's journey. These days my spirit soars with hope, peace, and serenity.

As a result of my healing, I became a practitioner of the healing arts trained in Reiki and Arcing Light. As part of my continued education in remembering who I am, my new path includes completing a master's in transpersonal studies, with the intent to eventually get my Ph.D. This will enable me to help others turn their lives around and to find their passion and keys for success.

Louise has been an inspiration in my life, and she's helped me lift my veils and take off my blinders. I am blessed to have found my way to her information. I still refer to her books *You Can Heal Your Life* and *Power Thoughts* on a regular basis—I feel so in tune with the connection and power they have over my own thoughts and life processes.

Thank you, Louise, for stepping out and putting your philosophies into practice, for without your shining light, I would not have been able to be who I am today. May the healing power of gratitude and love, along with the belief in a limitless world, bring us all together as one and heal the mind-body-spirit of each individual and the universe.

ﾞ ﾞ ﾞ

I Am Happy!
by Michael, registered nurse, Ohio

As a child, I was sexually and physically abused; as an adult, I continued to allow myself to be abused. I was unaware that my past didn't have to dictate my present. So if people showed me a little attention, I'd usually let them do whatever they wanted to me. My self-esteem was very low, and I didn't think I mattered. I didn't graduate from high school, and I went from job to job and from city to city in search of happiness, always falling short. I'd choose situations in which someone would hurt me just to validate why I was deserving of that pain, and then I'd sink into depression. I didn't know the power of my thoughts and that what I thought about most often, I became. It was a vicious cycle that kept me locked in my pain.

I'd always wanted to be a nurse, believing that if I could help others, then I'd feel better about myself. I did become a registered nurse and genuinely did like helping others. However, instead of feeling better about myself, I just became more miserable. The search for my happiness continued, and I kept on going from job to job, feeling horrible. Then one day someone told me about a woman named Louise Hay.

I listened to her *101 Power Thoughts* CD and read her book *You Can Heal Your Life,* and everything began to change. Suddenly, I didn't need to search for happiness in other people, or even in my career. I found happiness in *myself* because I began thinking, *Hey, I am somebody,* and *I love me!* My life started to turn around. Before I knew it, I became a nurse who not only loved others, but loved himself as well.

Since I encounter various people all over the country now as a traveling nurse, I have a large e-mail list in which I send out positive messages. I'm proud to help change the lives of the men and women I encounter through the words I speak. Yet if it hadn't been for that person who introduced me to Louise, I wouldn't be writing this story for you today.

As Louise has so perfectly stated: "It is only a thought, and a thought can be changed." That's how it began for me. I thought,

Hey, I can be happy. Now I *am* happy! I'm not perfect, but that's okay. Life is wonderful, and we can all experience the very best if we just allow ourselves to begin with that one single thought: *I can be happy!*

꙳ ꙳ ꙳

Affirming My Way to a Wonderful Life
by Katrina, student and part-time
retail sales assistant, Australia

In February 2008 my husband informed me that he would be financially better off without me and my two sons from my previous marriage, and he asked me to find somewhere else to live as soon as possible. I had no job, but the boys and I were fortunate enough to be able to stay with family members for a while.

At this point, the rental market was at its worst—I stood in massive lines of people to view the few available properties, to no avail. On my way home from one house-hunting attempt, I stopped at a bookstore and saw *You Can Heal Your Life,* by Louise Hay. I bought the book and read it in two days, vowing to give affirmations a try. Feeling that my attitude had definitely changed, I went back out to find a place to live. As I stood with 70 other people to view the same place, the agent from another property called to tell me that my application had been accepted, and the boys and I could move in within the week. All I could do was cry and thank God.

The next day, I noticed a "Help Wanted" sign for a part-time sales assistant's position at a fashion store I'd always loved. Again remembering everything Louise said in her book, I applied for the position right then and there—and I got it! This was proof that affirmations really do work! I'd prayed for a new home and job and visualized all being well in my world, and suddenly it was happening.

The boys and I moved into our new home, which is a mere two-minute walk from the store. At first, money was really tight because I hadn't received my first paycheck yet. I was to get paid on a Thursday, and we were down to our last tiny piece of soap on Tuesday. (Please don't get me wrong, I have a very loving and supportive family who would give us the world, but I was determined to do this alone.) When I arrived at work that Tuesday, one of my co-workers said, "Katrina, we all got a gift from a customer this morning who wanted to thank us for the service we give to her." Seeing the large basket of soaps the customer had brought us, I reminded myself that all of our needs are indeed taken care of, just as Louise states in her wonderful, life-changing book.

Tiny miracles continue almost weekly, from my tax return covering the entire amount of my car insurance to a refund arriving on the same day the water bill is due. But most important, my sons and I are happy and healthy and living in a nice place, and I love my job. We also have amazing neighbors, one of whom just finished the psychology course that I'm about to take. Yes, I've entered college and look forward to the new direction my life is sure to head in.

Thank you, Louise, for showing me the way to turn my life around. All is truly well in my world!

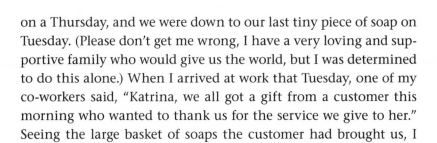

Life Outside of the Box

by Melissa, writer, photographer, artist, teacher,
attorney, and counselor of law, Colorado

When we speak of the miraculous, we tend to think of the unthinkable—larger-than-life, awe-inspiring events that defy logic or deviate from the laws of nature. Yet sometimes miracles come in tiny packages, imperceptible to the naked eye, like a slight shift in perspective. Like seeds planted in a fertile mind, they grow into a new way of being in the world, bringing extraordinary results for the one experiencing the change.

So it was with me. A lawyer by trade, I began my career at the age of 24. Conflict and struggle surrounded me, yet I ironically found the antagonistic nature of the legal profession (and business in general) quite troubling. I looked for answers outside of the box, knowing that there had to be a better way for me to navigate this left-brained world.

Along the way, a massage therapist recommended that I read Louise Hay's book *You Can Heal Your Life.* Soon I found myself studying a new kind of law: the universal laws of spirit. This was the first step in my personal transformation, a journey that brought into focus the power of positive thinking, affirmations, meditation, and prayer. After going through Louise's book, I read everything I could find that touched on the power of our thoughts and the laws of spirit, including many titles by Hay House authors. It wasn't long before I began to restructure my life.

Universal law was my bridge between two worlds. Although I had no delusions of being able to transform the entire legal profession, I understood that real change must begin within; then it can extend outward to our families, organizations, groups, cities, nations, and the world at large.

The more I studied and integrated these principles into my own life, both personally and professionally, the more consciously I connected with life. I shared my newfound wisdom with anyone who would listen, clients and colleagues included, and worked hard to be the change I wanted to see.

As they say, "From small acorns grow large trees." What started as a quest to understand the madness led me to pursue a unique path from which I emerged as a universal lawyer, an advocate and counselor of both "man's law" and the universal laws I write so passionately about (in my monthly wisdom column featured in a local magazine and on my blog).

Today my life looks very different. Now I move freely between the physical and spiritual worlds and the right and left sides of my brain, enjoying a career as a photographer, artist, creative writer, teacher, and universal lawyer. This is no small task for a girl once deeply entrenched in a very linear world.

Years ago, in the middle of a grueling negotiation, a client told me, "Miss Johnson, miracles don't happen." To him I respectfully said, "I beg to differ, sir."

Louise, thanks for your groundbreaking work and for showing me that I *can* heal my life . . . one thought at a time.

⚡ ⚡ ⚡

More Than a Survivor, More Than a Rose

by Jeannie, vice president of sales, California

My father was drunk again and putting a gun to my head . . . and you can imagine how the rest of the night went. Even though I was only 15 years old, I'd already experienced years of abuse of all kinds. I left home the next morning and never returned. I now consider that most horrible night a blessing, as it gave me the impetus to leave.

I turned out to be a good survivor, staying with the family of a friend from school for two months. Then I found a job at a theater, and a roommate to share an apartment with. I saved my money and bought a used typewriter from Goodwill, determined to get a job in an office and improve my situation. So I worked on my typing skills and lied about my age. I was able to get an office job, using the bus for transportation.

I learned everything I could. After passing my high-school-equivalency exam, I started college at night. Although it took me almost ten years, I eventually got my degree, a B.S. in accounting.

I may have been good at being a survivor, but I was poor at picking men—by age 40, I was on my own with four children. I wanted to do more than just survive, and soon attracted a book that changed everything: *You Can Heal Your Life*, by Louise Hay.

I began to affirm that I could have a great job creating money rather than counting it, and that I'd make plenty of it for all of my family's needs. Within three months, I was offered a job selling pumps, hard hat and all, and I proved I could excel at sales. My next affirmation was to sell products I loved and believed in. Not only did that opportunity show up (selling Hay House books!), but I've been very successful for the last 18 years. While I have a great job and a beautiful home, what's more important is that I know I am

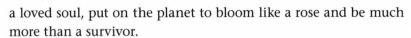

a loved soul, put on the planet to bloom like a rose and be much more than a survivor.

My hope is that I can share my story with young girls and boys so that they can see the importance of never giving up hope. Not only can they make it through their challenges, but they can flourish and realize how very much they are loved.

Doing the Work with Louise

Do you know what you truly want to do and how you truly want to feel? Don't answer immediately with the "right" answer, with what you think you're *supposed* to want and feel. Be willing to go beyond what you believe today, and consider what genuinely makes you feel alive and inspired. Then think of positive actions that will allow you to feel this way always. Be conscious of your thought patterns, and let go of old beliefs that do not support your better life.

The exercises below will help you figure out what you truly want, accept that you *do* deserve it, and welcome it into your life. Write your answers on a separate piece of paper or in your journal.

Think about What You Deserve

Answer the following questions as openly and honestly as you can.

1. What do you want that you do not have now? Be clear and specific about your desires.

2. What were the laws/rules in your home about deserving? Were you told that "you don't deserve anything special" or "you deserve a good smack"? Did your parents feel deserving? Did you always have to earn in order to deserve? Did earning work for you? Were you told that you were no good? Or that sinners don't deserve? Were things taken away from you when you did something wrong?

3. Do you feel that you deserve what you want? What is the thought that comes up: "Later, when I earn it," or "I have to work for it first"? Are you good enough? Will you *ever* be good enough?

4. Is there anyone you need to forgive in order to deserve what you want? Keep in mind that bitterness puts a wall around our hearts and makes it difficult for us to receive.

5. What do you truly deserve? Do you believe: "I deserve love and joy and all good"? Or do you feel deep down that you deserve nothing? Why? Where did that message come from? Are you willing to let it go? What are you willing to put in its place? Remember, these are thoughts, and thoughts can be changed.

Mirror Work

Look in your mirror and say, *"I deserve to have or be _____, and I accept it now."* Say it two or three times.

How do you feel? Always pay attention to your feelings, to what is going on in your body. Does it feel true, or do you still feel unworthy?

If you have any negative feelings in your body, then turn back to the mirror and affirm: *"I release the pattern in my consciousness that is creating resistance to my good. I deserve _____."*

Repeat this until you get the acceptance feelings, even if you have to do it several days in a row.

Creating Your New Life

What do you have to live for? What is the purpose in your life? Write a story about yourself having or doing or being whatever you are working toward. Fill in as many details as you wish about the things that fill you with passion and enthusiasm. Really let your mind get creative, and *have fun!*

Visualization

Next, see yourself actually living the life you just created in the previous exercise. What does this ideal life feel like? What do you look like? What do you feel, see, taste, touch, or hear? Imagine your relationships. Who are you associating with? Relax and breathe in your newfound freedom and happiness.

What Makes You Happy?

Now think about what would make you happy. This is not the time to talk about what you *don't* want. This is a time to be very clear about what you *do* want in your life. List everything you can think of. Cover all the areas of your life. List at least 50 things that would bring you closer to the ideal life you visualized.

After you've written every desire you can think of, write an affirmation next to each item. Create your own, or use one from the list below. You deserve to have a wonderful new life!

Affirmations

I release the need to be unworthy. I am worthy of the best in life and allow myself to accept it.

I have the power, strength, and knowledge to handle everything in my life.

My mind creates my experiences. I am unlimited in my ability to create good in my life.

My inner vision is clear and unclouded.

I easily flow with new experiences, new directions, and new changes.

I am open to the wisdom within. I am at peace.

I now surpass other people's expectations.

I am safe in the Universe, and all life loves and supports me.

I am willing to create new thoughts about myself and my life.

I am willing to learn. I move forward with ease.

*I bless each situation with love and know that everything
    works out in the best possible way.*

I am willing to go beyond my own fears and limitations.

I center myself in safety and accept the perfection of my life.

I respect myself. I am Divinely protected and guarded.

I see my patterns, and I choose to make changes.

I understand how wonderful I am. I love and enjoy myself.

I create a new life. I only accept beliefs that totally support me.

I believe in my power to change. I am willing to take the next step.

I live in the now. Each moment is new.

I create a wonderful life that gets better with each passing day.

Treatment for Finding Your Purpose

*I am one with Life, and all of Life loves and supports me. I am deserving.
I deserve all good. Not some, not a little bit, but all good. I now move
into a new space of consciousness where I am willing to see myself
differently. I am willing to create new thoughts about myself and about
my life. My new thinking transforms into new experiences. The totality
of possibilities lives before me. I deserve a good life. I deserve an
abundance of love. I deserve good health. I deserve to live comfortably
and to prosper. I deserve joy and happiness. I deserve freedom to be
all that I can be. I deserve more than that: I deserve all good! The
Universe is more than willing to manifest my new beliefs. This is
the truth of my being, and I accept it as so. All is well in my world.*

Afterword

Thank you, dear friends, for embarking on this amazing journey with me. To everyone who contributed, I am deeply humbled by your kind and loving words, and am honored that you took the time to share your experiences with me.

As I mentioned in the Introduction, the point of this book was to show you that one human being has the power to touch so many others in a positive way, so I hope you will do just that as you go about your daily life in the months and years to come.

Be a force for good on our magnificent planet. Spread love, joy, and compassion. Give when and where you can. Perform an act of kindness each day. Express gratitude to the Universe for all you are and all that you have. And most of all, know that you are worthy of love, prosperity, and all the other wonderful things Life has to offer.

You and I can make this world a better place . . . every day, in every way.

And so it is.

Louise L. Hay

50 million books sold,
50 million lives changed.

Embrace the change.

About the Author

Louise L. Hay, the author of the international bestseller *You Can Heal Your Life,* is a metaphysical lecturer and teacher with more than 50 million books sold worldwide. For more than 25 years, Louise has helped people throughout the world discover and implement the full potential of their own creative powers for personal growth and self-healing. She has appeared on *The Oprah Winfrey Show* and many other TV and radio programs both in the U.S. and abroad.

Louise is the founder and chairman of Hay House, Inc., which disseminates books, CDs, DVDs, and other products that contribute to the healing of the planet.

Websites: **www.LouiseHay.com®** and **www.HealYourLife.com®**.

To receive a free issue of *The Louise Hay Newsletter,* please call Hay House at: 800-654-5126.

Deep at the center of my being there is an infinite well of love. I now allow this love to flow to the surface—it fills my heart, my body, my mind, my consciousness, my very being, and radiates out from me in all directions and returns to me multiplied. The more love I use and give, the more I have to give— the supply is endless. The use of love makes me feel good. It is an expression of my inner joy. I love myself; therefore, I take loving care of my body. I lovingly feed it nourishing foods and beverages. I lovingly groom it and dress it, and my body lovingly responds to me with vibrant health and energy. I love myself; therefore, I provide for myself a comfortable home, one that fills all my needs and is a pleasure to be in. I fill the rooms with the vibration of love so that all who enter, myself included, will feel this love and be nourished by it. I love myself; therefore, I work at a job that I truly enjoy doing, one that uses my creative talents and abilities, working with and for people whom I love and who love me, and earning a good income. I love myself; therefore, I behave and think in a loving way to all people—for I know that that which I give out returns to me multiplied. I only attract loving people in my world, for they are a mirror of what I am. I love myself; therefore, I forgive and totally release the past and all past experiences, and I am free. I love myself; therefore, I live totally in the now, experiencing each moment as good and knowing that my future is bright and joyous and secure— for I am a beloved child of the Universe, and the Universe lovingly takes care of me now and forevermore. And so it is.

Notes

Notes

Hay House Titles of Related Interest

YOU CAN HEAL YOUR LIFE, the movie,
starring Louise L. Hay & Friends
(available as a 1-DVD program and an expanded 2-DVD set)
Watch the trailer at: **www.LouiseHayMovie.com**

THE SHIFT, the movie,
starring Dr. Wayne W. Dyer
(available as a 1-DVD program and an expanded 2-DVD set)
Watch the trailer at: **www.DyerMovie.com**

✴ ✴ ✴

Ask and It Is Given: Learning to Manifest Your Desires,
by Esther and Jerry Hicks (The Teachings of Abraham®)

An Attitude of Gratitude: 21 Life Lessons, by Keith D. Harrell

The Body "Knows": How to Tune In to Your Body
and Improve Your Health, by Caroline M. Sutherland

A Daily Dose of Sanity: A Five-Minute Soul Recharge
for Every Day of the Year, by Alan Cohen

Excuses Begone! How to Change Lifelong, Self-Defeating
Thinking Habits, by Dr. Wayne W. Dyer

Healing Your Family History: 5 Steps to Break Free
of Destructive Patterns, by Rebecca Linder Hintze

The Heart of Love: How to Go Beyond Fantasy to Find
True Relationship Fulfillment, by Dr. John F. Demartini

How Your Mind Can Heal Your Body,
by David R. Hamilton, Ph.D.

It's Not the End of the World: Developing Resilience
in Times of Change, by Joan Borysenko, Ph.D.

The Power of Infinite Love & Gratitude: An Evolutionary Journey
to Awakening Your Spirit, by Dr. Darren R. Weissman

This Is the Moment! How One Man's Yearlong Journey
Captured the Power of Extraordinary Gratitude,
by Walter Green (available October 2010)

What Is Your Self-Worth? A Woman's Guide to Validation,
by Cheryl Saban, Ph.D.

✈ ✈ ✈

All of the above are available at your local bookstore,
or may be ordered by contacting Hay House (see next page).

✈ ✈ ✈

We hope you enjoyed this Hay House book. If you'd like to receive our online catalog featuring additional information on Hay House books and products, or if you'd like to find out more about the Hay Foundation, please contact:

Hay House, Inc., P.O. Box 5100, Carlsbad, CA 92018-5100

(760) 431-7695 or **(800) 654-5126**
(760) 431-6948 (fax) or **(800) 650-5115 (fax)**
www.hayhouse.com® • **www.hayfoundation.org**

Ƙ Ƙ Ƙ

Published and distributed in Australia by:
Hay House Australia Pty. Ltd., 18/36 Ralph St., Alexandria NSW 2015 •
Phone: 612-9669-4299 • *Fax:* 612-9669-4144 • www.hayhouse.com.au

Published and distributed in the United Kingdom by:
Hay House UK, Ltd., 292B Kensal Rd., London W10 5BE • *Phone:*
44-20-8962-1230 • *Fax:* 44-20-8962-1239 • www.hayhouse.co.uk

Published and distributed in the Republic of South Africa by:
Hay House SA (Pty), Ltd., P.O. Box 990, Witkoppen 2068 • *Phone/Fax:*
27-11-467-8904 • info@hayhouse.co.za • www.hayhouse.co.za

Published in India by: Hay House Publishers India, Muskaan
Complex, Plot No. 3, B-2, Vasant Kunj, New Delhi 110 070 • *Phone:*
91-11-4176-1620 • *Fax:* 91-11-4176-1630 • www.hayhouse.co.in

Distributed in Canada by:
Raincoast, 9050 Shaughnessy St., Vancouver, B.C. V6P 6E5 •
Phone: (604) 323-7100 • *Fax:* (604) 323-2600 • www.raincoast.com

Ƙ Ƙ Ƙ

Take Your Soul on a Vacation

Visit **www.HealYourLife.com**® to regroup, recharge, and reconnect with your own magnificence. Featuring blogs, mind-body-spirit news, and life-changing wisdom from Louise Hay and friends.

Visit **www.HealYourLife.com** today!

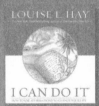

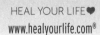

HEAL YOUR LIFE ♥

Take Your Soul on a Vacation

Get your daily dose of inspiration today at **www.HealYourLife.com®**. Brimming with all of the necessary elements to ease your mind and educate your soul, this Website will become the foundation from which you'll start each day. This essential site delivers the latest in mind, body, and spirit news and real-time content from your favorite Hay House authors.

Make It Your Home Page Today!

www.HealYourLife.com®